What people are

The Promise of Right Relationship

Wisdom makes room for simple truths to change us in the tiniest and most profound ways. Pamela Haines's life, as illuminated in these essays, speaks of the courage and joy of right relationships with the people and the natural world around her. *The Promise of Right Relationship* offers insights, inspiration, and delightful examples for all of us striving to live loving, conscientious lives. **Nadine Hoover**, author of *Creating Cultures of Peace, Walking in the World as a Friend,* and editor of *The Power of Goodness*

I don't know anyone who wouldn't find this remarkable book helpful: deepening their awareness of how they live their lives, increasing their confidence, sense of power and choice, and love for themselves and others. Pamela Haines' voice is calm and reassuring, with a gentle humor. I noticed more light in the room where I was reading. **George Lakey**, educator and activist, author of *Dancing with History: A Life for Peace and Justice*

Pamela's collection of essays is a series of reflections on topics most of us care about. She articulately describes what it means to be a seeker, yet also aware of her advantage in the world. She is always caring, always curious, and always sensitive to multiple perspectives. She manages to go beyond the simplistic good guy/bad guy narrative, lifting up nuance and coating it with love. Her specific stories all lead to a broader understanding of our world. Her essays left me feeling more joyful and more able to play my part. **Shelley Tannenbaum**, General Secretary, Quaker Earthcare Witness

Within the Judeo-Christian-Humanist tradition, Quakerism has uniquely centered the ethics of right relationship. Combined with the ethics of reverence for life, it lifts the veil on a flowering landscape of readaptation in which a social economy of adequate access to the means of life under the governance of "no more than needed" provides a bountiful and satisfying way of life. I am delighted to see Pamela Haines take up this theme in such a fresh and wide-ranging collection of essays. I commend them to the attention of all.

Keith Helmuth, author of *Tracking Down Ecological Guidance*

Previous books

Toward a Right Relationship with Finance: Debt, Interest, Growth, and Security
978-9768142887

Money and Soul; Quaker Faith and Practice and the Economy
978-1789040892

That Clear and Certain Sound; Finding Solid Ground in Perilous Times
978-1789047653

Alive in this World
978-9768273260

Encounters with the Sacred and the Profane
978-9768273345

Tending Sacred Ground: Respectful Parenting
978-1803410883

The Promise of Right Relationship

The Promise of Right Relationship

Pamela Haines

CHRISTIAN ALTERNATIVE
BOOKS

Winchester, UK
Washington, USA

JOHN HUNT PUBLISHING

First published by Christian Alternative Books, 2024
Christian Alternative Books is an imprint of John Hunt Publishing Ltd.,
No. 3 East St., Alresford, Hampshire SO24 9EE, UK
office@jhpbooks.com
www.johnhuntpublishing.com
www.christian-alternative.com

For distributor details and how to order please visit the 'Ordering' section on our website.

Text copyright: Pamela Haines 2023

ISBN: 978 1 80341 424 9
978 1 80341 425 6 (ebook)
Library of Congress Control Number: 2022946781

A CIP catalogue record for this book is available from the British Library.

Design: Lapiz Digital Services

UK: Printed and bound by CPI Group (UK) Ltd, Croydon, CR0 4YY
Printed in North America by CPI GPS partners

We operate a distinctive and ethical publishing philosophy in all areas of our business, from our global network of authors to production and worldwide distribution.

Contents

Preface

As I thought of how to begin this book of reflections, my mind returned again and again to Quaker John Woolman, who lived in the late 1700s on the eastern seaboard of North America. I can think of no other person who exemplifies the spirit of right relationship more fully. If he were to read anything I have written here and nod his head, I would be honored beyond words.

To John Woolman

Friend John,
pacing your apple orchard in colonial times,
pondering the evil that grows from love of money,
the plight of the poor, how they connect,
where we fit in.

Opening your heart to the oppressed —
field workers, beasts of burden
all who labor painfully that others might indulge
in that which only separates them from God.

Traveling long hours on horseback or on foot
to visit those who still hold slaves,
taking time to center first in love —
love for all God's creatures,
the least and the great,
the harmed and those who harm
(perhaps unknowingly)
then searching for the words
to open clouded hearts.

I feel you near. I read those quiet, careful words
and hear the great passion that rings beneath,
your keen mind revealed, undaunted by truth
unflinching in the task of bringing it to light.

Your mind's alive in me—
the choice to look and think,
make sense of our economy,
who works, who gains, how money flows,
puzzle out connections, patterns, probe for roots,
sure that life together here on earth
can somehow be made right.

Your single-minded quest
sounds the depths of courage
and of faith. I glimpse where you
in hard-won steadfastness believe:
we cannot be at peace
until our lives are stripped down to our share.

Your task is laid upon my heart.
If only you can find the words to say
how sweet it is to live as we were meant,
while willing us to look, clear-eyed
at all the facets of our unconsidered lives—
the excesses that weigh us down
the ease that rubs another raw—

If only you can stand before us one by one,
invite us through hard truth and through great love
to lay those burdens down—
then we will change.

Impossible, so it would seem—
or maybe not.

Foreword

Keith Helmuth

When I was working on our Quaker Institute for the Future book, *Right Relationship: Building a Whole Earth Economy*, I was thinking primarily of the subsidiary relationship of human economic behavior to the terrestrial and biospheric boundaries within which it operates, along with the social context of equitable access to the means of life, which extends to the whole commonwealth of life.

That's a pretty broad sweep, but when a friend spoke later of the "ethics of right relationship" it tripped my consciousness of the expression into a new appreciation of its reach and its functional utility as a framework of guidance. The experience was on par with my long ago reading the philosophical works of Albert Schweitzer and encountering his articulation of "the ethics of reverence for life."

In his quest for the foundations of ethics, Albert Schweitzer conducted an exhaustive and unsuccessful search through all the cultural systems and great philosophers of the world seeking a coherent basis for ethics. After being intellectually defeated by his efforts, he was opened to his cardinal insight while *not thinking*, but rather contemplating the teaming panorama of life before him on a river voyage from his clinic to another Congo village for the delivery of medical services. "Reverence for life" came to him as the state of consciousness in which a coherent and durable basis for ethical guidance can be found. He wrote that the "iron door" blocking his efforts had "opened." His quest, thereafter, was in the field of articulation and application, in mindful living.

The ethics of reverence for life, as articulated by Schweitzer, cautions us—no more than needed. "No more than needed," indeed! Try lining that guidance up with the growth-insistent economy and the destruction of earth's biodiversity that "normal" living now routinely requires. It's enough to make one weep.

The ethics of *reverence for life* and ethics of *right relationship* together lift the veil on a flowering landscape of readaptation in which a social economy of adequate access to the means of life under the governance of "no more than needed" provides a bountiful and satisfying way of life. This is not fantasy. We know this kind of readaptation works because there are examples of it that are flourishing and a movement for scaling up is underway. It's not about "simple living." There is nothing simple about it. It's about discipline and hard work. It's a calling to solidarity with the commonwealth of life in the interests of survival.

My experience, triggered by that phrase, "ethics of right relationship," was not so dramatic as Schweitzer's opening to "reverence for life," but it launched me into a realization that the concept of right relationship translated into a lens of consciousness and a tool of analysis that had the potential to become a cultural meme.

I have witnessed increased reference to "right relationship" over the last fifteen years. The emergence of "the ethics of right relationship" is one of the flags being flown ever higher over the consciousness of the readaptation required to stop the destruction of the commonwealth of life and create new systems of biologically coherent and socially equitable human settlement.

But more than a spreading cultural meme, "right relationship" is also a central concept in Confucian and Buddhist traditions, and is strongly evident in the respect with which many Indigenous peoples honor the whole Creation.

Within the Judeo-Christian-Humanist tradition, Quakerism uniquely seized on the "ethics of right relationship," which was brought to a fully rounded expression by John Bellers and John Woolman. John Bellers' economic and social justice thinking powerfully influenced Robert Owen, the founder of the Cooperative Movement. Bellers was cited by Karl Marx "as a veritable phenomenon in the history of political economy." John Woolman was also an observer and analyst of economic behavior and a proto-ecologist who saw and called out the wrong relationship of not only slavery but of landowners who degraded the fertility of the soil by maximizing short-term wealth accumulation.

Of course the rise of "right relationship" to the status of a cultural meme did not come *sui generous* into the Quaker lexicon. It is rooted in a variety of contexts, which extends the range of its recognition and increases the subtlety of its penetration to both the cognitive and emotional levels of ascent. I think it fair to say the way "right relationship" rose within our work with Quaker Institute for the Future appears to have helped stir a remembrance among Friends and seed a resonance that is now self-propagating, which is what an effective meme does.

I am delighted to see Pamela Haines take up this theme in such a fresh and wide-ranging collection of essays. I commend them to the attention of all.

Keith Helmuth is the author of *Tracking Down Ecological Guidance; Presence, Beauty, Survival.*

Introduction

The issues of our day are big ones (to say the least!): human rights, racial justice, economic equality, democracy, the climate. It's easy to be moved by the passion of those who are active in movements for change, to be inspired by their words and actions, unite with their vision, and feel that they are speaking on our behalf. But right relationship requires more. Passive agreement is not relationship. Relationship requires showing up.

Of course the ways of showing up are infinite, differing for different people, times and circumstances. We can throw ourselves in fully, claiming this as our work. We may be leaders ourselves, or build on our experience to identify decision-makers and offer insights on what will make their work most effective. We can find a group that is working on this issue and join in. We can find someone who has chosen to be involved, and offer them consistent encouragement and backing. We can make a point of staying informed in ways that allow us to thoughtfully amplify a message. We can open up personal conversations with friends and family. We can hold the goals and those who are actively engaged in our hearts. What we can't do, if we value our integrity, is not show up at all. Being in right relationship requires discernment. What is a role I can play that is a fit for my circumstances, my gifts, and the situation and needs of the other? Do my reasons for being involved or not involved stand up to testing? It requires staying close enough in to know if/when our relationship might need to change. Whatever role we find, being in right relationship also requires being an open-hearted peer, neither desperate to have personal needs met nor assuming that we know best, but ready to both give and receive.

These great movements of our times cry out for such discernment. But there are other parts of our lives that call for right relationship as well, and sometimes the ones that are closer in can be harder to see with a clear eye. How do we find our way to right relationship with ourselves and our own goodness and failings, with those around us and what we need, with knowledge and mastery and work?

As I reflect on questions that might aid in discernment in all of these areas, I think of the principles I was raised with in my Quaker community. We called them "testimonies," but they might be more accurately described as frameworks for living: community, equality, simplicity, peace, stewardship and integrity. Is the community around me nourished by this choice of a way of being? Is equality both embedded in the position I am taking, and promoted as a goal? Is it essentially simple? Does it cut through the layers of complexities and clutter in modern life and expose the clean lines of truth? Is it life-affirming? Does it acknowledge my place in the larger community of life and my responsibility to nurture it? Is it honorable? Does it have the ring of truth?

The times are tumultuous. The situation we find ourselves in will continue to change. There will be no final decision about the form that our response will take. But an intention to keep reaching for right relationship will be integral to helping us find our way forward.

1

Goodness & Falling Short

Fine and well

When I was growing up, the dominant story line was that we were a big happy family, that everything was fine. With little hard evidence to disprove it—and much to support it—I accepted this worldview as truth. Since we were all fine, and my mother was very busy working to keep it that way, how could I complain? So I settled into the job that had been laid out for me of having a happy childhood, and more or less succeeded.

What a shock to discover as an adult that my childhood hadn't been as happy as I had been taught. It turned out that my father was harsh and judgmental, my mother had deep emotional needs, and in a family that prized education I secretly (even to myself) hated school. All in all, it had been quite a chore to be the hard-working non-complaining responsible team member that my big happy family required.

Realizing that everything had NOT been fine was a huge relief. I took some time luxuriating in outrage at what I'd had to put up with, and began flirting with the idea of complaining. Yet I was constrained by the awareness of how relatively good my life had been. To increase my confusion, the life I was living in the present was a marked improvement over my childhood, and as my perspective on the ills of the world widened, my own little problems seemed more and more petty and insignificant.

At the same time, I fought against being pushed back into that familiar position where the needs of the larger whole always and inevitably trumped mine. Did I, or did I not, have a right to complain? I started experimenting: complain about this, complain about that. In a way it was a relief to be able to notice and say out loud that some things did not feel fine. But it was confusing. Were my complaints real? Were they from the past or the present? Was I really not fine? Though I liked the possibility that there could be space in the world for my complaints, did I want them to define my emotional state?

Yet I couldn't go back to fine. In reality, everything had not been fine in my family, and everything is certainly not fine in the world. The attempt to believe or pretend that it is requires walling off great pieces of reality and agreeing to a small and defended life. While I was born into relative comfort and have more than enough in the present, it's not hard to notice that I'm in a minority. Our peoples and our planet are in great and growing distress, and I ignore that reality at peril to my soul.

In a real way, "fine" has no substance. Used as a response when people ask how you are, it's clearly just code for "I'm choosing at this moment, for any number of reasons, not to complain." It's no more than an opaque brush-off.

I'm reaching for a response that captures more truth. Currently this is how it sounds, in three parts: "I have a few complaints." There is space in this world for me to experience life as I experience it, and things will not all be sunshine. "There is a lot to grieve and fear." I am connected to the larger picture, and I would choose to engage with all that is not fine rather than turn away. And, finally, "I am well." I have found my way to a life of connection, joy and meaning, even in the midst of great suffering, and will not be rocked from that place.

In my experience, being fine calls for a cover-up, as completely as possible, of all that is wrong, and a commitment to construct a life on top of that cover-up. Being well is the opposite—a commitment to connecting to the solid ground that lies underneath, and engaging with all that is wrong, and all that is right, from that place. I am happy to consign "fine" to the dustbin of history, and have great faith that "well" will see me forward.

Taking up space

I had found the last seat in the back of the trolley and was idly watching as a pleasant-faced young man worked his way in my direction. He found a friend across the aisle and as he turned to chat, I saw his backpack barely miss the head of an old man sitting in front of me. Every time the trolley swayed and the young man moved to balance, the backpack moved too. In horrified fascination I watched as it swayed away from the old man's head, then came back closer, bumped lightly, swayed away. The old man hunched forward. The friends' conversation continued uninterrupted. The pack swung. Finally, I could stand it no longer and called the young man's attention to what he was doing. He turned immediately to apologize, and adjusted his position. Clearly, he had been unaware. He apologized again as he left the trolley, and I should have been satisfied to let it go.

Yet it stayed. Somehow that backpack had become a symbol for me of all the well-intentioned people in this world who take up more than their share of space, and are cosmically unaware of their impact on others. It has stayed with me as well since this issue of taking up space pulls me hard in two very different directions.

On the one hand, I have a goal of taking up more space in my life. If you think of all of us having a certain allotment of space in this world—the exterior of our bodies, how far our arms and legs extend, the air space around us, I tend to be pretty conservative. I can squeeze into a small bit of a bed or a couch, am pretty quiet in groups, and spend more time in my interior than on my borders pushing boundaries and bumping up against others. Yet I think it makes sense to venture out from the safe fortresses some of us have built deep inside. It makes sense to explore our frontiers, live out to our very edges, inhabit the places where we overlap with and bump up against others.

I think that's the only way to be our full selves, to be as big as we were meant to be. And, for a conservative like me, that might mean risking the mistake of taking up space that isn't mine.

On the other hand, it is painful to see the unawareness with which people fill up space that doesn't belong to them, or that clearly needs to be shared. I am particularly conscious of the space that wealth takes in this world, the resources it uses, the size of the footprint it leaves on our earth. I would not wish to take up so much space that others are left without enough. And I think we, in the richest country on earth, do that all the time without even knowing it. We're certainly not trying to hurt anybody. And, unfortunately, the solution is not as easy as taking off the backpack and stowing it between our legs. But I think we have to start by noticing, and by being willing—if only in principle at this point—to be content with our share.

So, I'm left with the challenge of stretching all the way out to my edges (and maybe beyond at times, if that's what it takes to find them) and, at the same time, of not taking up more space than is mine. It sounds impossible, but I have a hunch that if we all rose to the challenge, we would find that there is enough for everybody—maybe not to have all the stuff we are used to, but to stretch and breathe freely and have a big life.

Outside the law

I'll never forget the little boy on our street who, when asked to pick up a snack wrapper he had dropped, defiantly replied that his mother let him litter. While many of us may have an ambivalent relationship to the law, I'm not sure I'd ever heard such an unapologetic decision to live outside of it—and can't help but wonder what laws he flouts as an adult.

Beyond attempts to live outside the letter of the law, there are others who defy a less clearly defined social contract—the expectation that everybody will grow up, be responsible and do their share of the work. They tend to cluster in two extremes:

those who cannot find their way into the social contract because of inequity and oppression and respond with various kinds of lawlessness, and those who have access to enough money to buy their way out.

Their experience outside the social contract is very different. Those with too little who have broken criminal laws are pushed into an incarceration system that seems increasingly intent on barring such people from equal participation in society forever. Those with too much often drift untethered outside the circle, roaming from one adventure to another, bedeviled by the irony that, when anything is possible and nothing is required, choice itself loses meaning. Yet this individual freedom, the right to do anything we want, unconstrained by limits, is held out as the ultimate good in our society.

This is deeply problematic, since we are all subjects of another big law out there—natural law—that we didn't create and can't change. We have been lulled into assuming that the earth's resources and the atmosphere's capacity to absorb waste had no end. We have been confused by the discovery of fossil fuels—an ancient layer of compressed plant life—into believing that energy supplies are unlimited. We have assumed there was an "away" into which we could throw things. We have relied absolutely on technology to dismantle every limit we encounter. We have been trying to live outside the natural law since the dawn of the Industrial Revolution, but are facing its ever more unavoidable requirements.

This is a hard transition to make. We have channeled our narrative of living within the law into harsh punishment of the smallest infractions by the most marginalized people. (Perhaps it's not surprising that those whose violations are breathtakingly bold and outsized—damaging tens of thousands of lives in high-stakes gambling on home mortgages, or avoiding billions of dollars of taxes in complex off-shore schemes—get a slap on the wrist, if not a pay-off.)

One way of reshaping the narrative is to embrace the challenge of living within, and being constrained by, natural law. The possibilities are endless. Explore all the other options to cool yourself before turning on the air-conditioner. Do without foods that have traveled thousands of miles, and cultivate a taste for what's local and in season. Stand against the pressure to buy new when what you have will still serve. Get somewhere without a car. Practice savoring each tiny taste or moment of a luxury, so you don't need much to be satisfied. Think of this not as privation, but as a series of victories in finding joy living within the law.

Of course, individual change is not enough. Those who are rogues when it comes to the law of nature need to be stopped, and standard legal and political remedies will likely fall short. Nonviolent direct action—which challenges the political law, but is prepared to abide by its consequences—is a promising way of pushing our current system from the inside to reshape its boundaries.

As I reflect on it, there is something about that little boy's distain for the letter of the law that resonates with the rebel in me. But I resonate more deeply with restorative justice practices, where nobody is ever pushed outside the circle. It is so clear: as members of the community of life on Earth, we all belong within the circle of its law.

Scapegoating and blame

Our conversation on scapegoating started with the treatment of Jews. For centuries in the West, Jews—an easily identifiable minority with a strong cultural bent toward learning—have been used by those in power as their up-front agents, especially as money lenders and bankers. When the economic or political situation sours, their vulnerable minority status allows them to be named and targeted as the problem, providing an outlet for the pent-up anger and frustration of the populace, while shielding those with real power.

We have created an "other" to whom blame can be assigned. Punishment has been meted out, the problem has been contained, and life for the rest of us can go on. While the Holocaust was perhaps the most calculated and certainly the most horrendous manifestation of this type of scapegoating, the examples are legion, and the impulse to blame the Jews has burrowed deep, if often unconscious, into our common psyche.

I hadn't done much more systematic thinking about this dynamic, but a friend who was a child in Germany during World War II raised the issue of Germans as scapegoats. People who take a stand against the barbaric treatment of Jews under Hitler can easily fall into seeing the Germans as the problem. How convenient! If we can assign the blame for anti-semitism to the Germans, we are off the hook. We have created an "other," the problem has been addressed, and life for the rest of us, now rendered blameless, can go on. In a very similar fashion, an image of Germans as the bad guys has burrowed deep.

It becomes obvious that the same dynamic is at work around racism. Those of us who live in the North in the United States can be easily seduced into a belief that true racism resides in the South. Having created an "other" and assigned the blame, we are off the hook about racism, and can bask happily in our more evolved goodness.

Clearly scapegoating has many uses. It channels dissatisfaction away from the real issues, thus supporting the status quo and obstructing change. It provides a safe target for venting our feelings. It helps us avoid painful truths by freeing us from the responsibility of considering our part in the situation. We can use it to jack up our sense of our own goodness.

As we considered the overlap between scapegoating and blame, the conversation got more personal. Could we survive without blame? How often do we assign blame in a situation of disagreement or conflict, and see that as an adequate response? What if we actually had to *do* something? Are we willing to confront our part in the situation, face our complicity, and decide to be different? Could we find a way to do that without blaming ourselves?

The challenge is full of opportunities. If blame is not an option, then situations just have to be faced for what they are, which allows for ways forward to be found. If no one is to blame—neither me nor, most commonly, my partner—then no one can be consigned to the status of "other" and the task is simply to find a path out of this less-than-ideal situation. Even when I feel that the other person is totally in the wrong, if I can vent without targeting and take the lead in finding a blame-free way forward, I'm the one who gets to grow.

Then the conversation broadened back out—way out. "Maybe," said one young woman, "this is why I haven't found a way to be involved in social change. It seems like it's all about finding bad guys and pointing fingers." Ultimately, blaming the bad guys, even the ones who are wielding the real power, won't help either. Yes, they need to change, but scapegoating and blame are ultimately the tools of the insecure. An infinitely more powerful approach mirrors the way a loving parent sets a limit with a small child. "I'm not going to let you do that, sweetie." There's no blame—just compassion for the person hidden behind that bad behavior, and great confidence that things can be different.

I think we all left with our minds atingle. I certainly went away newly excited about the possibilities of a world without blame.

Goodness and neglect

I neglected my backyard last summer. There were perfectly good reasons for it, and I'm not second-guessing the choices I made that had it low on my list. But the longer I neglected it the harder it became to choose to pay attention. I felt bad about that neglect, and facing the result of it was painful.

When a blessedly open day arrived in October, my feet finally took me out the back door and down the steps. What an unkempt jungle! The clouds of tiny white flies on the kale in my little kitchen garden were the worst. How could I have been so irresponsible in tending a living thing that was under my care? I found myself doing everything else except getting out the detergent spray for that tedious job. I realized that I was mad.

I was mad at the need for all that work—but mostly I was mad at the image of myself that was reflected back to me. So the flies, and the kale that had attracted them, got the brunt of it.

Once I could notice that I was directing my anger at that innocent kale, my mind actually got a little space to think about this phenomenon. I doubt I'm the only one. Why do I get mad at what (or who) I care about and don't treat well? I think it's because I would choose to believe that I'm a good person, and what is reflected back to me calls that into question. To protect my goodness, I blame the one I've treated badly.

It's logical, in a twisted kind of way. And it makes me wonder how much this dynamic underlies neglect and abuse in many other places. How many people who treat loved ones badly have fallen into a pattern of responding to their own less-than-thoughtful behavior by lashing out at those with whom they have fallen short? How many people in privileged social positions defend what they haven't earned by finding fault with those who have less?

I'm happy to say that while there's still more do to, my backyard looks 100% better. It reflects well on me, and my eyes can now rest there in pleasure. I'm no longer mad at the kale, which I did finally get to spraying that afternoon (though I notice that it could use a second treatment now).

Perhaps most important, I have a personal and visceral understanding of how easy it is to try to protect our goodness when we're in the wrong by projecting that wrong onto others—

and how easily that can lead to even more neglectful and hurtful behavior.

In my heart of hearts, I know that I'm not a bad person. Perhaps my next step is to go out and just apologize to the kale—then give it another spray.

Taking sides, taking stands

I've been thinking recently of an old labor song with the refrain, "Which side are you on, boys, which side are you on?" Are you with the hard-working folk who are risking their livelihood— and sometimes their lives—to stand up for their rights, or are you with the greedy, unscrupulous fat-cat owners? As I used to sing that song, I felt connected to the courage of the downtrodden and warmed by the assurance that I was on the right side. Yet over the years I have become increasingly uncomfortable with the question itself.

It is everywhere. Are you on the side of the earth or with those who would heedlessly ravage it for short-term gain? The abused or the abusers? Democracy or tyranny? In a way, it's all one question: Are you with the good guys or the bad guys? Our sports teams are by definition the good guys, as are our armies, and life certainly seems sweeter when they win.

We come to this investment in being good guys on the winning team from a host of deeply-felt, and often painful experiences growing up. School is full of taking sides. We choose—or are chosen, or not chosen—for teams where winning is everything. We join—or are excluded from—social groups that help define who we like and don't like. Many of us have even earlier experiences in our families—needing to be on one parent's side, or one sibling's or with children or the grown-ups. Or our ethnic or racial or class or religious identity in a divided society requires us to be part of a side. We have been pushed and shoved and cajoled into a world of side-taking from the very beginning.

I don't believe we are wired this way. Our earliest experience of taking sides grew, rather, from a scarcity of options. I don't think we chose freely as little ones—it just seemed that there was no other way. It was painful when others chose against us and it was painful to choose against others. Somehow our fears about our goodness, perhaps about our very survival, have become entangled in the choosing and occupying of sides.

But what if the whole concept of opposing sides is flawed? And what if there is enough goodness to go around? What if there is always something beyond our side or theirs? Those who are quick to take sides, or are passionate about their identity as good guys, have little patience with this possibility, seeing those who refuse to take sides as weak fence sitters, lacking principles or courage, ultimately pawns of the bad guys. Yet, while there could always be cowardly motives for refusing to make a hard choice, I see courage in daring to challenge the whole frame.

As we begin to see the web that trapped us all when we were growing up, and step away from the sides we felt required to take, the world starts to look different. The bully gets our attention as well as the victim. Both the protesters and the supporters listen carefully to the others to fill in their picture of reality. We discover that everybody cares about the earth.

Of course this means taking stands. It means mobilizing energy toward our vision for the future. It means saying, "This behavior is not right and must stop." But it doesn't demonize. It doesn't require a framework of good guys on one side and bad guys on the other, and a willingness to embrace people from opposing sides is critical to our survival.

2

What We Need

Enjoying enough

When we have easy access to more than we need, how can we enjoy what we have, and how can we tell when it's enough? Few of us believe that a fabulously wealthy person needs one more excess to tip him from dissatisfaction to happiness, yet we haven't worked out that equation for our own more modest lives. And the work of recognizing "enough" may be more important than we know, as we come up against the limits of our planet's resources.

I've been noticing recently how this plays out for me with food. When I stepped on a scale recently, I was dismayed to see a number I hadn't seen since pregnancy. Usually, I set aside a quiet week or ten days in the summer for very disciplined eating to lose the weight that has accumulated over the year. But I didn't get around to it last summer and I definitely indulged over the winter, so I started my eating discipline earlier than usual, with a bigger goal.

Part of me wants to be rigid and put absolutely no carbs or sugars into my body, and get that weight down fast. Yet I find myself experimenting. Somebody bought some tasty-looking crackers and left them invitingly on the kitchen counter. So I filled a tall glass of water, took one little cracker, went to the office, and proceeded to eat it, very slowly. It *was* tasty—every single tiny little bite. I felt like I'd given myself the full cracker experience, without sacrificing my goal. The same has been true for chocolate chips, my main sugar indulgence at home; a single one can provide a powerful long-lasting chocolate taste. Four chocolate chips in a day, enough to fully satisfy my craving for indulgence if experienced fully, won't set me off track.

Even though the quantities are much smaller, I am getting the same amount of enjoyment out of things that I love—or maybe even more—simply by putting more attention to enjoying them—and I'm losing weight! I have to wonder: could this be true for other people and in other parts of our lives? Of course it's easier to see our excess weight as a problem that we're motivated to do something about than our excess shoes, for example, or excess stuff, or excess hours of being entertained. But I think the principle is the same.

If we can't pay attention to enjoying what we already have, then going for more is probably a waste of resources—because we'll keep seeking fulfillment through the getting rather than the enjoying, and it will never feel like enough. This is bad for our own well-being and, multiplied by millions of fulfillment seekers, bad for the future of our spaceship earth.

Some people in this world don't have enough to lead decent healthy lives, and they really do need more. But for most of us, the path to feeling like we have enough lies more in our attitude and where our attention goes than in greater consumption. Maybe we'd actually be helped by more scarcity—if there's only a little bit, then our only path to happiness is to enjoy it a lot!

Ownership and repair

I have been puzzled over the years by how tenacious I get in mending torn and broken possessions. Sometimes it seems ridiculous. Why not, for goodness sake, just throw them out and get something that will work?

It has occurred to me that there is a bigger issue here, of relationship and service. When I buy something new, it serves me. I am in the relationship of master or mistress to that possession. I have it at will. I have placed some value on the service it can provide me, and expect it to serve me well. If it ceases to play the role I expect of it, there is no reason not to replace it with something that does.

Once I start repairing, however, there is a relational shift. Now that my time and skill have gone into making that thing whole again, the relationship is more one of peers. It serves me, and I serve it to the best of my repairing ability. Sometimes it doesn't do as well as I would wish, and sometimes my repairs are wholly inadequate—and I am the one found wanting.

While I have many other stories of this dynamic that are longer and more complex, the brown sweater provides a simple example. Relatively new (to me) it has been, if not a favorite piece of clothing, a serviceable addition to my wardrobe. When I noticed a seam that was coming undone, I took a few minutes to make a neat repair, glad for the skill that made the task so easy. Later it was more seams, a small hole in the back, and a missing button. This repair took a little more time, and more ingenuity. As I studied it for anything I might have missed, I felt a new sense of connection. This sweater had a new lease on life because of my care, and I cared for it more as a result.

As I mend more, I care more. The challenge then becomes when to acknowledge that something I have cared about has come to the end of its useful life, to find a way to dispose of it fittingly and mourn its loss. The acquisition of a replacement is bittersweet, and brings with it all the weight of a new relationship.

But I have no regrets. I would rather have all the responsibilities of a give and take relationship, when I sometimes do well and sometimes fall short, than be in the role of master, surrounded by servant/slave possessions that exist at my pleasure and are likely to be discarded at the first sign of frailty or imperfection. Sometimes, I have to admit, it can feel like I'm running a nursing home, and it can be a relief to let one of them go. It certainly can be lovely to have something new that works to perfection. But I'm still glad to have the skills to prolong so many good and useful lives, and I would never want to give up that sense of connection, and all that opportunity to care.

Turning the collar

This was a favorite shirt. When the elbows wore though years ago, I cut them off and transformed it to short sleeves with minimal fuss. (And then I had the pleasure of using the sturdy fabric from the lower arm and cuffs for quilt squares.)

But when the collar began to fray, it wasn't so simple. If I didn't do something it would soon be suitable only for wearing around the house. But if I put a patch over that frayed spot, I still couldn't wear it to work in an office downtown.

Then I remembered the possibility of turning the collar. People used to do it all the time. After all, back then, how could you imagine abandoning a perfectly good shirt if just one side of the collar was showing some wear? Surely I had the skills to pull this off?

Once the idea entered my mind, it took root. I waited impatiently for a time when I could justify turning away from "more important work" to engage in such a luxury. After all, I do have other shirts. I looked at it many times lying there on the worktable between the computer and sewing machine, and itched to see what could be done.

Finally, a window opened. I found my scissors with the tiny sharp blades, perfect for cutting thread, and got to work, carefully snipping the collar loose from the rest of the shirt. It wasn't hard at all. Later I stole a few minutes at the machine to sew it back on the other way, with the frayed part now invisible underneath. I could have left it at that, but this good shirt called out for better treatment. So I found a bit of bias tape, and once again waited till I could justify taking the time to make a neat little patch.

The mend was now complete. The shirt could be worn to work again without concern. And I was pleased. In fact, I was extremely pleased — more pleased than a simple mend should warrant. I kept looking at it, folding that fine new collar down, running my finger over the unfrayed fold, turning the collar up to see the patch that would be visible to no one but me.

Why such inordinate pleasure? As I sat with this question, it came to me that it has something to do with claiming my connections in space and time. It connects me to our ancestors who knew the value of a well-made garment. They turned collars as a matter of course, turned dresses, mended cleverly and invisibly if possible, and neatly if not.

It connects me to our neighbors as well, to those who have less means in the present and know the value of a good mend. I remember seeing carefully mended dress shirts in Africa, and being touched by the attention that people took to looking neat in the midst of poverty. And some of my most satisfying excursions when visiting our son in Nicaragua involved shoe repair. More than once I brought down old shoes that would be discarded as worthless in this country. At the market, however, we always found men who saw the value of those shoes and were glad to use their skills to make a sturdy and serviceable mend.

It also connects me to our descendants. The time will arrive when we finally come to our senses and realize that we are living beyond our ecological means, when—willingly or unwillingly—we in the wealthier nations adjust our lifestyles to a level that the planet can support. When that time comes, a good shirt will have a value that may be hard to imagine in our present-day orgy of consumption and waste. Looking down that tunnel of time, I can see our descendants turning the collars of their shirts once again—and I will be with them in spirit. I just hope it might give them a fraction of the satisfaction and pleasure that it has given me.

Rethinking security

A few years ago, I had the opportunity through work to meet a lovely family who run an early childhood program in a poor part of the city west of where I live. I liked them a lot and was glad they were interested in having some of the tomato seedlings I had brought to the meeting to share. We talked a little about the garden they were hoping to start and later that month, I dropped some kale and collard seedlings off at their center.

I stayed in touch and arranged to have them host one of our early childhood meetings the following spring. We had another long conversation about gardening, and they showed us the little raised beds they had built in a big empty lot down the street. Seeing that expanse of empty space, I spent time over the next several weeks separating perennials in our community garden, and starting a little ad hoc nursery of flowers, vegetable starts and fruit bushes to share.

Then on a Saturday morning in May, I worked together with them for three hours, hauling dirt, arranging and planting vegetable beds in the sunny back, and putting all the flowers in a couple of beds out front where they could be enjoyed by passersby.

I came home with new friends. He shared a jar of his famous homemade barbeque sauce with me, and I'm looking forward to going back and giving him a jar of my currant juice and a recipe for currant sorbet. I'd love to see if we can get some hardy perennials to take hold in the vast rocky middle of that lot. Mostly I'm looking forward to being friends together.

As I meditate on this experience that has given me so much pleasure, it occurs to me that it can also be seen as an investment in my long-term security. In a neighborhood that was easy to think of as other, I now feel a deep point of connection. My world is safer, my extended family has been extended and enriched—and I now have a source for fine barbeque sauce!

This is not money in the bank in the traditional sense, and by itself it won't support me in my old age. But there's a way in which it may be equally valuable or more so. It may make as much sense to put time into building these human assets as it is to working extra hours to save up money for an individual future. These connections are a critical part of the picture as we struggle to find our way in this "now and not yet" world.

Comfort and judgment

My partner and I had a difference of opinion about how to get a crowd of folks up to his brother's farm. We would fit in two cars, but it would be more comfortable and convenient to take three. Since it was his birthday celebration, I didn't press the point. Three cars were, indeed, very convenient, and the impact on the planet of those extra hours of car driving was barely worth noticing in the larger scheme of things.

The part of the conversation that stuck in my mind, however, was our interchange about comfort and judgment. When I said that I wasn't a big fan of arguments based on comfort, he said that was easily seen as judgmental, particularly by those for whom comfort has been scarce. I felt painfully torn. One of the dearest wishes of my heart is to leave behind forever the spirit of judgmentalism that pervaded my childhood. Yet I also can never forget a little card that my mother had posted above her desk: "Convenience pollutes."

All the disposables—the plastic, paper and foam of fast food and picnics, diapers, paper towels, juice boxes—made to be used once and thrown away; those quick errands where driving can save so much time; the second car that avoids having to take the public transportation schedule into account; the pre-processed, pre-cut, pre-packaged food that is so much quicker to prepare; the washer-dryer in every house and the lawn-mower in every garage; all take a toll on the earth's resources and capacity to absorb waste. There's no doubt: convenience does indeed pollute.

I'm thinking now that comfort also pollutes. Year-round climate control, big luxurious cars, that long hot shower in the morning, the freedom from having to be jostled by crowds, first class airplane seats, golf carts—the list could go on. A love of comfort has its own traps in terms of what we will trade away for it. Feeling *entitled* to comfort elevates the problem to a whole new level: who would I fight to hang on to what I have come to believe is rightfully mine?

I do believe that comfort has a place in this world, as when someone is sick, or dying, or grieving a great loss, or when someone has exerted enormously. Coming from the root of the word, "to strengthen greatly," it is an appropriate response to particular circumstances, a mechanism to soften adversity or make a time of challenge more bearable. But I baulk at the conclusion that most of us in the industrialized west live in such a state of chronic challenge that we require round-the-clock comfort.

Also, if we have it all the time, if we come to expect it as our due and make sure it's always present, then its utility as a means of softening adversity is lost. It has become the new normal, and something more comforting, more comfortable must be found to take its place. I'm troubled by the implications of this dynamic of escalation—on our psyches, on our connection to others with less access to comfort-providing resources, and on the health of our planet. I much prefer a bracing level of discomfort, so we can better appreciate and truly luxuriate in our comfort when it comes.

But what about judgment? Theoretically I could just learn to respect everyone's different decisions around comfort. Yet I find myself unwilling to concede, unwilling to completely surrender this territory to personal choice. I don't see a lot of clear thinking here, with all our wounds and insecurities making us so vulnerable to the lures of comfort. Add in a multi-million-dollar comfort-selling industry, and it's hard to make truly free choices in this area.

My mind jumps to the deep desire my young children had for the junky plastic toys that surrounded them—on television, in the stores, in the hands of their friends—and how mad I got at their upset when those toys broke. It was a struggle to be on their side at these moments, but I finally found a way to be true to both of us. "I'm so sorry," I would say, "that the people who make those toys just think about money, and don't care about what it feels like for children when they break."

Maybe I can learn from that hard-fought victory to be on the side of people who seem to be choosing short-term comfort over their long-term psychic well-being and the overall health of our biosphere. "I hate it that this issue of comfort is such a loaded one. What a confusing mix of different personal preferences, standards, levels of adversity (past and present), histories around discomfort, takes on what's due to us and to the future. Add in a system that is squeezing out sources of real comfort, like time with loved ones, and focused on convincing us we need and deserve any product or service they can make a buck off of—and the chances of having a relaxed and mutually enlightening conversation on this topic recede toward zero. But I want to try. I want us to be on each other's side as we puzzle this thing out together."

3

Work

Wired

I was at my mother's house, way out in the country, and my car wouldn't start. She suggested that I consult a friend who knew mechanics. He agreed that all signs pointed to the starter motor, advised me where to get one, and said he was sorry he was too busy to put it in himself. I was sorry too.

Three minutes later, as I was perusing the Yellow Pages for a tow, he called back. The delivery of his turkeys had been delayed. He had time to work on the pens later, and would be happy to put in my starter motor. The best time would be right now, before chores.

I heaved an enormous sigh of relief and took my mother's car off to town to buy the motor. I came back to find his truck already in the yard, his head under my car. I brought out lemonade, stuck my head under the car to keep him company, offered an extra hand, and listened, learning something about car repair, and a lot more about his farm.

When he wiped his hands and said, "That should do it," the car started up as if born to it, and I wondered how I could possibly repay him.

Money was out of the question. So I offered to help on the farm. As he was washing his hands, he said, "Well, we're pretty behind in our vegetable garden..." Now that is something I do know about, so I completed the deal before he could reconsider.

The next morning, I started the car again—what a gift!—and drove through sparkling sunshine and green and gold hills to spend a couple of hours creating order among his onions and carrots and beets.

I don't think we are wired as human beings to sell our gifts or our time. I think we are wired to do work that we love and to share with those around us.

Work and love

I've been a worker all my life, and never imagined how anything could be more satisfying than doing a good piece of work. But I'm starting to see its limits—noticing how I can choose to work from a place of love, then have that love fade into the background as I end up just moving through my days with steady resolution.

I don't want to escape from work, but to transform it, to bring the love into the foreground. Perhaps the impetus comes from having recently cut back my hours of paid work, or maybe there's something about this pandemic that encourages a focus on what really matters. Probably it's a combination of both. I also realize that I'm coming from a position of privilege, not needing to focus most of my attention on survival. But I'm ready for more.

To bring love into my work, I've had to start with my to-do lists. I'm a master here. I'm good at creating them, good at moving through them, and the feeling I get when I put a line firmly through a completed item is enormously satisfying. One more thing off my list is one step closer—to what? The end of the day? A new day with a new list? Is my life an endless series of lists, stretching out before me to eternity?

I guess this is where theology comes in, the hope for a reward in heaven. But, while I absorbed the Protestant work ethic into my very cells, Judgment Day was not part of my upbringing and has no resonance for me. What I have instead is that small, sharp satisfaction of crossing something off my list.

How could I imagine an alternative to that endless string of lists? How could I organize myself—my days, my work, my hopes and dreams—into something less linear? What if, instead, my life was a web, fastened by long strands to realities that were firm and true, with me in the center? What if other strands connected me to those I love? What if my life's work was defined by keeping all those strands and connections strong, while throwing out new lines to weave an ever larger and more resilient web?

The challenge has become to realign my days from a list of tasks to a web of love. Rather than writing down a series of to-do's, I've started putting people's names into my web. The tasks that had nobody's name lived uneasily at the edge of the web for days, till I realized that I could name anchors that hold the ends of the strands: I love my community; I love the world. The trip to the credit union could be identified by the name of a renter, whom I'm glad to have in my life. The tasks I have taken on for the public banking campaign can be defined by the people associated with those tasks. Then I saw that by naming other anchors—I love the earth, I love to create—things I would never think of as tasks, like sewing while on a call, or being in the garden, can have a place in the web as well.

Puzzled at first by how to keep track of progress without just crossing them out—assigning them to history with that sharp stroke of a pen—I now cover them with a little heart. There are still unsolved puzzles. Tasks that I haven't particularly loved, like housecleaning, can fit in the newly-named strand of loving my home, but what about the taxes? I block out time for work and appointments on the same page, so I don't lose track in these long days at home, but how might they fit in the web? What about my email, which can be an overwhelming tangle of news from loved ones, things to do, interesting information, and requests for support, all clamoring for attention? What can I move from my mailbox to the web? I'm discovering that the simple act of putting something in the web lifts a sense of burden and adds a reminder of connection.

A straight line that stretches on to eternity can certainly evoke respect, direct one's feet forward, and gratify a sense of order. But a web is a closer match to how life is organized. And a web is something to love.

Carrying our load

Living in this world, it's easy to feel overburdened. How can I discern what is fine to carry on my shoulders, and what is unrealistic, or unfair, or too much, or just not my responsibility? Recently, after completing years of hard work in a leadership position in one group, everyone just assumed that I would pick up leadership in another place that had need—because they knew I was capable. It made me mad. After several months of stubborn resistance, I realized that I actually had a vision for how to accomplish that piece of work, very different from how it had been done in the past, and exciting to me. I offered to lead if the group would join in my vision—which they did. Having found a way to freely choose from a position of power, my whole attitude about the work involved was transformed.

There's a lesson here about choice, about taking off of our shoulders the responsibilities that don't belong there (put on us by others when we were young, or assumed because there seemed to be no other option), and taking on what we choose in the present, based on our best thinking, our abilities, our love, and our vision for the future.

Then there are situations where we find ourselves with too much on our shoulders in the present and no way to refuse to handle it—the result of forces totally outside our control. In these situations, the big lesson for me is about getting help (a key missing ingredient when I was young). I would guess that one of the biggest difficulties many of us have with taking on responsibility is in imagining the possibility of getting the help we need.

I've recently realized that my feelings from childhood of being totally alone with tasks that seem too hard can get me into trouble. At times I feel so overwhelmed by a challenging demand that I try to avoid it altogether—like not even opening a letter from some intimidating bureaucracy. I'm trying to remember now, as soon as I recognize that familiar sinking feeling, to reach out and break the isolation, then do what needs to be done.

Maybe we all need to check what we're carrying, dump out some of that heavy weight that doesn't belong to us (like trying to make our parents happy), and pick up some of the pieces that lie waiting to be done. If we can remember that we have the power to make adult choices and get help in the present, everything looks more possible. I do believe that we all can find our way to carrying our piece of the world's responsibility gladly, and without chafing at the load.

Reclaiming labor

The shovel digs into the pile. After twenty-seven pushes and lifts, abs and arm muscles working, the big wheelbarrow is full. It's enough to mulch five or six feet of path. Each trip, from the pile of wood chips in the parking lot, through the gate of the community garden, down the narrow path that separates the front flower bed from the vegetable plots, gets a few feet shorter. The November day is warm. The red of the setting sun shines in the windows of the houses along the street, each trip from a slightly different angle. The wood chips are fragrant. It takes about twenty loads in all (I wonder how many lifts of the shovel). By the end my muscles are protesting—but what a satisfying job!

The next week I read in the paper that, along with $48 for cell phones and $40 for cable TV, average monthly expenses for Americans now include $59 for gym membership. We work long hours to afford labor-saving devices on the one hand and gym memberships on the other, when real work is out there, waiting to be done.

I can imagine how wasteful my labor must have looked. Certainly some device, a fork lift-type automatic mulch spreader could have been invented (or maybe already has) to save my muscles all that hard work, so I could be privileged to use them at expensive specially-designed muscle work-out machines at the gym. (I remember a friend wondering how much better off we all would be if everybody got out every morning and swept the sidewalk in front of their house. We'd get the exercise, the fresh air, the experience of community, and free cleaning, all at the same time.)

A good carpet sweeper works as well as a vacuum cleaner but you have to put a little weight into it. A push lawn mower requires the push. Stirring a cake by hand does work that arm. An errand on foot or bicycle can get the heart pumping. Why have we decided that this is bad? How is it that our lives will go better if we exert less energy?

Somehow labor has gotten a bad rep—as something people do if they're not smart enough to work with their brains, or rich enough to avoid work at all. Throughout the ages greedy rulers, slave owners and industrialists have been—and still are—happy to use people up and throw them away. Long hours of hard physical work have worn people down, worn them out. Perhaps the experience of generations has worked its way into our psyches; our desire to be saved from labor has assumed mythical proportions.

Yet what are we being saved for? Theoretically we could conserve that energy and turn it to something that we care more deeply about. Some of us have chosen for exercise. So long as there is no smell of work, so long as it doesn't accomplish anything, we will exert to the utmost—run, lift weights, climb rock walls or mountains. Probably more of us are seduced by the societal message that relaxation is the ultimate goal, and end up squandering our saved energy in front of the TV or restlessly searching the malls and the internet for well-being.

Exertion and relaxation are two halves of one whole— and somehow, we are being short-changed at both ends. Our culture is our enemy here; our labor-saving economy is enslaving us anew. It offers too few ways to exert our bodies that produce results that matter, too few forms of relaxation that provide true rest. I would choose to do more shoveling, pulling, lifting, sweeping and stirring—and more just sitting on the stoop watching the lightning bugs and welcoming the night.

Observation and accountability

A group of early childhood educators was struggling to imagine an ideal system for recognizing and funding high quality programs. One the one hand, we noted that much of what has the greatest value in human communities is not easily reduced to metrics and measurements. On the other hand, the stewards of public dollars need some assurance that they are not pouring money into black holes. How can a young child's well-being and growth best be measured?

One woman, who comes into preschool classrooms to help them improve their quality, argued passionately for observation. If a teacher can learn the skill of observing each child closely in all the domains of their development—social-emotional, academic, physical—she will surely be able to speak with authority on how they have grown through the course of a year.

While we didn't come to a final solution on what would satisfy the politicians who control the dollars, we found ourselves on increasingly solid ground in terms of accountability—and the word "observation" stayed with me. It rang with that clear and certain sound of truth. This woman is helping teachers learn to see, and it's clear that the underlying motion is love. There's power here, in developing the capacity to observe with love, and to act on what one sees.

While our conversation was about early education, this power can be found anywhere. I think of the farmers who observe their land closely, in the context of love. They learn its composition and needs in different times and places, and see what interventions allow it to flourish over the course of time. They consider the condition of each particular bit of the land—soil type, drainage, sun—and see themselves as partners in building up its capacity to support life.

Both these teachers and these farmers feel some particular responsibility for their environment—and both feel empowered to act on its behalf. They see strength and build on it; they see readiness and offer opportunity. They study signs of trauma, abuse or neglect for information that can help them shape the most targeted, compassionate and nurturing response. They hold out a vision and act, in a context of close observation and love.

This is very different from laying on an externally-generated development plan, like implementing a canned curriculum followed by standardized testing, or pouring in prepared inputs (the most potent seeds, fertilizers and pesticides) and measuring results per acre.

How might this understanding play out in our communities? What does a close loving observation reveal? We look for the things that give us joy, and soak them up. We notice the strengths that are there to be built on. Just as with a beloved child who may be challenged or troubled, we rejoice in what is whole and right even if that may not be the first thing that catches the eye.

Then comes the harder part: looking straight at where the community is traumatized and broken, just as the teacher looks at the child who is struggling, or the farmer looks at a crop that is stunted. They don't avert their gaze, or assume that the work belongs to someone else or they are not big enough to do what needs to be done.

Of course, a person could argue that it's very different with our communities—and could probably win the argument if they tried. Few of us, after all, are in a formal position of leadership in the world around us. The buck does not obviously stop with any of us, as it does with the teacher who runs the classroom or the farmer who "owns" the land.

And yet, I think the win would be a hollow one. It would have to be based on a commitment to not look, to not love, to stay small. So, I'm throwing my lot in with observation. What do I see? What do I see when I really look? What agency do I have to build on the strengths that I observe? How can I align my life and my efforts with life's unquenchable urge to flourish? What powers are available to me—powers of imagination, or organizing, or growing, or networking, or healing, or mending, or modeling courage—that could help make our world more whole?

Escape

Two narratives of escape were colliding in my brain. I was reading an account of life in the conflict regions of east and central Africa, including harrowing stories from people who had escaped conflict to a refugee camp in a neighboring country. At the same time, many of my co-workers had taken advantage of a conference in Orlando to escape from the daily grind and visit Disney World. They were worlds apart and totally different, of course. Or were they?

What do I know about escape? As a woman, it's been easy to notice how many men seem to use sports as an escape. I've sometimes wondered if the energy and passion they put into being on top of the sports news is a safer alternative to being on top of the much more troubling news of the real world.

It was a humbling moment when I realized that I had my own gender-based escape in reading feel-good novels. Other women choose shopping, or immerse themselves in pop culture, becoming experts in the lives of others. With more gender-neutral choices—many of them involving screens—the impetus is similar: I want out of the real world and into a place where I have no responsibility and can be sure that nothing problematic will intrude.

Then there is escape that is less benign. Many try escaping seemingly intractable problems—poverty, oppression, pain—through drugs or other damaging addictions. Which brings us to those refugees who were escaping for their lives.

Clearly it would have been better if the people in the refugee camp had not had to flee, if the perpetrators had not committed the initial atrocities, if they could have been stopped. Indeed, some in the camp were among those people, trying to escape from what they had done, wondering if they could ever be whole again. Similarly, it would be better if those who escape to dangerous addiction could find another way, if the resources could be found to deal with the pain or if their other needs could be met. In both situations there is immeasurable and tragic waste.

That's all very well, you may say, but where do sports, fiction, shopping and Disney World fit into this grim picture? By all appearances, they are totally different. Our lives are not ruined as a result of such escapes. On the contrary. We have simply laid down the yoke of obligation and given ourselves a little break.

But what does a need to escape say about the lives we are living? What are we escaping from? Could it be related to some basic lack of connection or meaning? Could it be something that is killing us? I can't help but wonder, if we were more closely connected with those refugees, whether we would see our choices in a different light.

When is escape an expression of our power and life-affirming determination—as in escape from abuse or confinement into a future that is different and better? And when is it the opposite—an expression of lack of power, a coping mechanism for endurance in a life-draining situation that we can see no way to change?

I wonder if we can make a clearer distinction between refreshment and escape. Let's be refreshed by all means. Let's take the vacations that invigorate us, rest deeply when we need rest, do what's needed to get a new perspective when ours is getting stale. But let's question the pull to escape. Let's ask what we are escaping from, then try deciding to stay, to gather the resources to face down the dragons, and put our energy into looking for real meaning and joy in our lives and those of others around us.

Midwifery

A regular high point in my weeks is being in touch with a handful of young activists from a youth climate movement. Through a young man who stayed in our spare room while doing student fossil fuel divestment work then went on to be one of the founders of Sunrise, I met another young woman on their Pennsylvania staff, who introduced me to still others. Just getting to know these lovely and deeply committed people is a joy in itself. Being able to be of use to them is an honor.

I think of one of the young women with whom I now do weekly hour-long calls. We have developed a little routine. We start with self-appreciation, since it's so easy to put all our attention on either our mistakes or the things we have not yet been able to accomplish. Then we exchange listening time, reviewing our emotional state and focusing on whatever we can vent or let go of to free up more attention and flexible thinking in the present. Finally, we check whether there's a puzzle she's facing at work that needs solving, or a knotty problem that needs untangling.

Often there's some small thing. She describes the situation. I listen closely, and ask questions to clarify. What does she want? Where does she feel on solid ground? Even if there are things she isn't sure of, is there a piece of the puzzle she is able to hold out with complete confidence? What is a doable next step? What is the right time, and who are the right people to go to with it?

It's clear to me that I don't know the answers. There's so much I don't know! Their organizational structure, which is complex, has never been described to me. I'm not exactly sure of her job description or her relationship to decision-makers. I'm not an expert in the types of campaigns they are running and certainly can't name the strategies that will allow them to succeed.

But I can provide an open space for the problem to be considered. I can ensure that this space is appreciative and free from prescription or judgment. I can listen and probe for what rings true. I can play the role of midwife. And more often than not the labor is quick and painless and the solution slips right out. What had been a worrisome muddle in her mind has become clear enough that she is ready—often eager—to take a confident next step.

Sometimes, of course, the problem is not one with a solution that is easy to think through. People lose track of themselves and each other in the midst of oppression and stress; they bring old and dysfunctional patterns of taking over or going quiet to their group interactions; old feelings of discouragement or desperation or self-blame gum up the works. There is time to tend to these issues in the middle section of our meeting, with attention to feelings of anger, fear, or grief that need to be released so that more space to think can be opened up.

This young woman, and the others that I listen to, are among the full-time staff of a movement that is mobilizing tens of thousands of young people in an effort that may play a critical role in securing a future for our species on this planet. As I do what I can to keep them working well together toward their goals—to increase clarity, restore confidence, amplify thoughtful voices, avoid missteps, seize opportunities, maximize the impact of scarce resources, strengthen relationships—I choose to believe that my small acts of midwifery are part of the labor process to bring a new world to birth.

4

Mastery

Becoming experts

The spring before my toddler grandson moved to Nicaragua, I loved taking him out to our community garden, and spending time just being present to the world around us. We smelled the flowers, dug in the dirt, watched the birds flying around, and listened to their songs. He was paying close attention, and the more he looked and listened, the more he took in. As he started to pick up language, among his first twenty words were bird, flower and smell.

Another toddler I know got interested in cars at an early age. He noticed, asked questions, took in and sorted new information, asked more, and now, at age three, can name every make and style as he walks down the street. This phenomenon of people becoming experts at what they pay attention to is everywhere: people who listen to the news each day and know everything about every bad thing that is happening; people who refuse to listen to news, but watch sports instead, and are experts on every team and every player; people who follow the celebrities and know every detail about their movies and their private lives; people who pursue a hobby and become experts in their own little realm.

I think there's an issue of power here. In a big world awash in information, it's nice to feel like you have mastery over some little bit of it. On the other hand, we can easily give up on whole areas where we despair of mastery. If we don't know anything about it, can't find a handle on it, we're not likely to choose to pay attention to it.

There are areas where we've gotten the message that we don't have aptitude—science for some, arts for others—and areas that we are actually discouraged from investigating. "Pay no attention to the little man behind the screen," says Oz the Great and Powerful... I think of the economists who turn away any question or criticism of their models and policies with proprietary warnings that they must be trusted, that only the experts can be expected to understand.

Yet, despite any obstacle in our path, we can still decide to grow into our own unlikely experts. The bottom line is that we get to choose where we put our attention. We can attune our ears and eyes to what we want to become experts on, knowing that it's possible to get ever better at what we pay attention to.

If time is a limiting factor, we may choose to withdraw attention from one activity in order to put it on another. Since I don't want to be an expert on despair, I don't watch the TV news. Since I do want to be an expert on what gives people hope, I have found ever more places to look, and take the time to look attentively.

What if we chose to pay attention to, and become experts on, that which makes us whole? In choosing to put attention on my place with our neighbors in this ecosystem that we share, I am coming to learn the birds. I am no expert. Far from it! How to pull discreet sounds out of background noise that I often don't even notice, much less to connect those sounds with a shape and a name, seems like a daunting task. But I also know that the choice is mine. If it's important enough to me to know my neighbors, I can decide to pay attention, and that blur in the background will begin to resolve into recognizable living beings.

I miss taking my toddler to the garden, but I'm glad to have played a role in inviting him to put his attention there. And the other morning I heard a new bird call, and for the first time in my life, could put a name to that bird.

A courage project

You can have fear without courage, but you can't have courage without fear. As I've been thinking about how we can best support each other to do scary things, I realize that we can take a lesson from the children. They look for activities that will test them—climb a tree, walk through a culvert, jump across a gap, have an adventure in the dark, tell scary stories. Children are pulled to test their courage, in a heady mix of fear and excitement.

As adults, some of us still thrive on risk; others are more cautious and prefer our thrills well buffered. Both tendencies are being increasingly accommodated by our consumer economy. Those who want risk without protection gravitate toward extreme sports. Those who prefer to consume it safely have a range of manufactured thrills available, from parachute and bungee jumping to amusement park rides.

It's a paradox. On the one hand, we are protected from risks in small things as never before; on the other hand, the big dangers we face are unprecedented. These are times that call for enormous courage about things that are real—the courage to face threats to our future, to welcome chaos, and to find our way together into the unknown.

I thought a lot about courage at a recent day of action on climate change, when I ended up stepping away, at the last minute, from risking arrest. Rather than going on auto-pilot to do what seemed "brave," I found myself choosing a path where I could stay more present and connected to myself, while still being involved in the action as a whole. As I reflected on this experience, I realized that there are many ways of being brave, and my most courageous act had probably taken place several days earlier: after noticing that I had been very quiet about my plans, I spent an evening daring to share with a wide circle of friends both my passion for the earth and my feelings about the action. Showing myself fully: now that's scary!

Courage is not one size fits all, and nobody can take another person's courageous step, but we all can be braver in ways that are completely our own. What if each one of us did a personal inventory of the times and places where we have been brave, and brought them to our community for acknowledgment and celebration? Then we could look at where our fears keep us quiet and passive, and develop personal courage campaigns. With a buddy or a small group, we could share our intentions to practice being brave—in our families, at work, with our neighbors, in the larger community—and come back to share our successes, or grieve our failures, and get ready for the next courageous step.

What are mine? Talking about what matters to me even though others don't seem to care. Openly trying a response, even though it might fail. Letting others know what I'm trying, and inviting them to join me. Once they've agreed, then sticking with it, holding out confidence that any second thoughts or complaints (theirs or mine) are just a way of showing our fears.

At a recent workshop on easing the transition to lower energy use by building resilience at a local level, the leader asked if anyone had the courage to build a core group that reflected their diverse urban neighborhood. I was surprised at her use of that word, but raised my hand. I'm not good at it. It's not coming quickly or easily. But I know what it takes to put my hand on the phone, think of a million useful things that I could do so much more easily than call somebody who is not yet in my circle, or who doesn't yet know how much I care about something that may not be on their radar screen, pause, breathe deeply, then make the call—and, when I don't hear back, then make it again.

We don't know how courageous other people are. We don't know what it costs them to do things that might seem easy to us. But together we can all do more. I'm looking to recapture that model from our childhood: A gang of buddies coming across—or setting up—a challenge. An open acknowledgment of fear: *Yikes, this is scary! Do you think we can do it? I don't know. Let's try anyway. Okay, here goes!* The squeals of excitement/fear, the shivers running up and down our spines, the uncontrollable shaking. Then assessing the results together: *Wow, we did it! Wow, almost, let's try again! Wow, that didn't work at all! What next?* Could there be a more human way of being in this world together?

Mastering creation

Human struggle for dominion over creation has reached epic proportions. While we have demonstrated a staggering capacity for mastery, the damage to the world around us has been staggering as well—and it's becoming increasingly clear that we won't have the last word.

Time at a shared cabin in the woods of northern Pennsylvania has provided lots of opportunities to consider who's in charge on a more intimate level. Sometimes we witness forces that are totally beyond our control. During the multi-year gypsy moth infestation, we watched helplessly as those little caterpillars ate up our woods. Great maple trees died and then fell, opening up sunlit spaces for briars and new young saplings to move in. Other trees survived, but took years to regain any semblance of health. Less dramatically, a rocky area of poor soil that had once been grazing land for sheep was still open and sunny when we arrived, with dozens of wild blueberry bushes. Gradually, with nothing eating off the vegetation, it has converted to scrubby woodland, and the blueberries have died away.

At times we have been able to nudge nature a little in the direction of our wishes. One year, when briars seemed to be steadily encroaching on the open area around the cabin, I found a dozen or so tiny little hemlock volunteers and transplanted them to form a barrier. At eight or twelve inches tall, they could initially be only a symbolic statement of how far we would protect our domain of human civilization, but each year they grew taller, and now tall trees form a barrier that is real.

The most vexing area of contention over mastery has been the pond. We human beings want it to stay as clear, clean and deep as possible, while natural forces are moving it steadily in the opposite direction. Created by others before we got there, with a small stream feeding it at one end, and a modest outlet at the other, it has little flow. Silt collects, pond weed gets more and more of a hold, cattails flourish at the edges and expand steadily inward. Everything that dies ends up on the bottom, and every year there is more organic material to grow and die.

We have tried many things: Spread chemicals on the water to kill the pond weed—but nobody really wanted chemicals in the pond. Import specially bred fish to feed on the bottom. This sounded like a winner—but in a year or two there was no evidence that they had made an impact or were even still there. Just keep unclogging the outlet, harvesting the pond weed and piling it up in great heaps in the canoe; wading in at the edges and pulling out armload after armload of cattails. This has probably had the most impact, but it's pretty clear that the forces of nature are stronger than us, and we haven't figured out any way to get the muck off the bottom without a massive dredging project.

Do we have a right to the pond of our dreams? This question took on more poignancy for me after reading a loving description by a Native American botanist of the richness of a cattail marsh, while all I could see was an obstacle in my path.

Then I think of our community garden, where we bring in soil, plant seeds in bare ground, define some plants as weeds and pull them out, offer extra food, water and supports to others that wouldn't manage on their own, wage eternal battles against bugs. We are totally bent on mastery; yet without some effort in this direction we wouldn't eat.

How to reconcile this conflict? Maybe we can learn from the farmers who know and love their land. They know the different soils, patterns of water absorption and run-off, sun and shade, woodland, marsh and field habitats, sources of soil replenishment, what part each plays in the health of the rest. With such intimate knowledge, with a sense of connection and belonging, with deep respect and thanks for the gifts of the land, I think we can see ourselves as partners and beneficiaries rather than masters.

Our pond struggle, I imagine, will continue. But perhaps I can approach it with more love, and if I pull out a cattail, I can thank it for the role it plays in this universe.

Teaching, learning, knowing

I love learning. It's exciting to go places and learn everything about a new environment—the culture, the history, the land. I love languages—the process of decoding an unfamiliar alphabet is a thrill. I can't imagine any craft that I wouldn't feel privileged to master more thoroughly. I'm passionate about understanding how social, natural and economic systems work—and how they could work better under different conditions. What makes people tick is endlessly fascinating, and the more I learn about how to play a useful role with other human beings, the happier I am.

Yet if there's one thing I can't stand, it's being taught. Having to listen while somebody expounds on something in my direction is torture. It's hard to think of a training I've attended that hasn't made me impatient. Being confined to a desk with an authority in the front of the room is a sure recipe for irritation. Of course there are explanations—bad school experiences from the past rearing their ugly heads, poorly designed lessons, expounders who don't really know that much. But what if being taught is just not always the best way to learn?

I've been struggling with questions of learning and knowledge as the group of people I work with — early childhood educators — are being required to go back to school in order for their programs to be rated of adequate quality to receive state subsidies. Many of these women are gifted in their work with children, yet that gift has no easy way of being acknowledged, so it is without value in this developing system. I rail against the injustice of it, against the incredible burdens of extra time and work that are being placed on skilled, hard-working and already-overstretched women. Why can't their competence just be recognized?

Yet some of these women speak of the value of the experience, the sense of accomplishment and pride that they feel, their excitement about taking new ideas back to their programs. Am I wrong?

I go to a conference on prior learning assessment, higher education's attempt to attract older workers with skills and experience by giving credit for some of the things they have learned on the job. It's a good step, but I'm still mad. What about the core of this job that makes all the difference yet cannot be taught in even the most advanced early childhood course — a loving heart?

As I make my way through this conference, however, stories from all over begin to form a pattern. Over and over again I hear that it is not easy for many people who have had no higher education experience to articulate what they have learned in life, to tease out what they know and how they apply that knowledge. Many struggle to think in terms outside of what it takes to get the job done. But when they understand that they possess complex bodies of knowledge that can be applied in a variety of settings, a new world opens up. They see themselves differently; they stand a little straighter; they can imagine that more is possible.

Ah. Self-knowledge. Reflection on one's role in the world. Now those are things I would want for everybody—even if it means some sacrifice. I still stand in opposition to a belief that more classroom hours logged measures greater mastery of a skill. And I'm still passionate about having a system that recognizes and appreciates those who are gifted, skilled, and knowledgeable—regardless of how they got that way. But I'm ready to support efforts that help anyone reflect on what they know, widen their horizons, identify what they want to learn, and get access to opportunities to learn it.

Ignorance

I've been wondering recently whether a greater appreciation of our ignorance might shine a light on the pathway to wisdom.

A friend led off a workshop on race and racism not long ago by asking participants to rank themselves as beginning, intermediate or advanced on the issue. It's an intriguing question. I think I would have said that I'm sufficiently advanced to know what a beginner I am. A few years ago, I might have claimed the rank of advanced. After all, I've learned history, puzzled over theory, built a wide variety of relationships, done lots of emotional work, helped others engage with the issues.

Since then, however, I've taken a deep dive into the nitty-gritties of racism in an urban farm project that has had to address thorny issues of Black spaces, reparations and community control. I am deeply grateful for that very painful opportunity, and have learned much in the process. I believe I knew enough to play a role that was more positive than negative, but am amazed at the extent of my naivete and blind spots. There is no way I can avoid my ignorance.

This is hard to admit. In my family growing up, ignorance was viewed as a terrible thing. Right answers were prized, and intellectual ability was encouraged above all else. My parents thought of themselves as outside of the mainstream, but I now see these values of theirs in complete alignment with the beliefs of the Enlightenment and the Scientific Revolution that have shaped our culture for hundreds of years: The pursuit of knowledge is the noblest endeavor; with it we can master the world. Ignorance is the enemy.

Yet where has this perspective led us? I recently came across a book, *Earth in Mind*, by David Orr, that is eloquent on this subject. Ignorance is not a solvable problem, he says. Rather it is an inescapable part of the human condition. Knowledge, on the other hand, is a fearful thing. He reminds us that to know the name of something traditionally was to hold power over it. Misused, that power would break the sacred order and wreak havoc. Why, I wonder, does that ancient warning ring so eerily true in our present condition?

He suggests that we cannot say that we know something until we understand the effects of this knowledge on real people and their communities. If we are too smug about the explosive increase of knowledge in modern times, we may fail to notice the knowledge that is being lost, and the critical nature of that knowledge for the survival of our species. We have broken the world down into billions of discrete knowable bits, but are lost when it comes to understanding what makes it whole.

Examples of the flaws of putting all our eggs in the knowledge basket are everywhere. Children are pushed to learn letters and numbers ever earlier, yet long-term success in school correlates more closely with a foundation of love of learning and strong social-emotional and problem-solving skills. Business schools turn out graduates who have aced classes on finance, planning and management, yet industry is desperate for the intangible qualities of leadership and entrepreneurial spirit. Scientists have mastered mixing chemicals to increase crop yields (at least temporarily), yet know virtually nothing about what creates soil health.

What would it take to decouple knowledge from hubris and from the blindness that seems always to come with it? Can we find the humility to accept our ignorance, to assume that anything we learn will illuminate bigger areas of unknowing that were previously invisible to us, and to cultivate an attitude of wonder at the unknowable? Perhaps then we can exchange the goal of mastery through attainment of knowledge for the ability to ask the questions that get to the heart of the matter.

5

The World

Generosity and invisibility

I was listening one morning to a Black man talk about helping a group of white folks address racism. Someone had said that we white people shouldn't expect Black people to help us out all the time, explaining things to us, getting us to see what continues to be so invisible to us. We need to learn to do it for each other. He said that, while it wasn't his responsibility to help, he had decided years ago that communicating his rage about racism in such situations made nothing better for anybody. By focusing instead on how he could help, he was able to respond to white people's blundering ineptness with power and grace.

Almost immediately after that conversation, in a different experience of invisibility, my husband was biking through Center City and was forced off the road by a big car. The driver was talking on a cell phone and never even saw what he had done. My husband's first response was pure anger at an unawareness that could have killed him. His second was a wish that he would never be as oblivious as that driver. He would choose to see what was going on in the world around him, even if it hurt.

We all want to be seen. At the same time, there are many things in this world, including the generosity of others, that are invisible to us. A friend was telling me of the role he has played in a political group all year—consciously backing the man who anchors and leads the group, bringing warmth and attention to the meetings, maintaining a hopeful and positive tone, making sure that people had fun together. He had chosen to play that role; he was glad to do it. But he struggled with its invisibility.

Everyone loved the group, but no one considered that there was effort being expended in making it go so well.

He said that maybe he was learning something of what it's like to be a woman, quietly tending to the needs of the group, intuitively knowing the importance of that work, but weighed down by the total lack of recognition.

And so I thought of the Black man who had decided to be generous with white folks. And I wonder which was harder — his decision to choose generosity over rage, or the invisibility of that choice to those around him. It had certainly been invisible to me. I had liked him, appreciated his accessibility, rested in the lack of guilt or blame I felt in his presence, but I had not seen what lay underneath.

So, I am challenged on both fronts: to be generous in the face of unawareness; and to see and more fully appreciate the generosity that comes my way. I like the idea of being generous, and not needing my issues or feelings to take center stage all the time. As a woman, I find that my life goes better when I act on the basis of my love and best thinking around men, rather than focusing on how I'm being treated. Yet I find it difficult to know when a decision to be generous in the midst of unawareness may not be a good one.

I know that if the loving source of my choice or the importance of my work is so invisible that even I can't see it, we all lose. If I am clear, it may not matter if the recipients of my generosity see it or not (and I certainly don't want an open-hearted impulse transformed into a stratagem for extorting appreciation). At such times I can look for support or a place to be seen by others who have made similar choices. At other times it will make sense to look for ways to address the veil that obscures the recipients' eyes, inviting them to clearer sight.

We are most likely to not see when we are in the positions of greater social power. Much of women's work is invisible to men. People of color stretch in ways that whites rarely know. When we are required to look, it can be painful. I have a working-class friend who is very aware of class issues and refuses to be invisible. I chafe at her insistence. Yet since I would choose to be seen, I would choose to stretch to see others and see how my behavior affects them. I would choose to be prodded to grow. Otherwise, I stay part of a power dynamic that degrades the quality of all our lives.

I particularly hope that I could take in the loving choice of a man who has a right to be angry and has decided to not direct that anger at me. If I am content with invisibility, I have unaware access to that man's generosity. But I can't know him fully. I can't learn from his struggles. I can't make use of his light to illuminate the parts of my life that remain obscure. I can't give thanks for his gift.

Claiming the history beneath our feet

It has been good to learn a little more about the people who lived in this part of our country before colonization. Their short name means "the people." Their longer name means "the true people." Their society was based on matrilineal clans, with land held in common by the clan. They raised maize, or corn, hunted in the forests, and fished in the waters of this watershed where I now live. With the arrival of the Europeans, there was a period of relatively peaceful interaction with colonists of relative integrity, followed by the ugly trajectory of history that we are familiar with: death by infectious disease and conflict, broken treaties, ultimate transportation to a reservation far away. Those who remained went underground, hiding their identity to avoid persecution, and blending in so successfully that they and their story were easy to forget.

Just before learning all of this, I was in a new city, and found a walking history brochure on the neighborhood I was in. It described change on different blocks over the last 150 years. Poor housing giving way to rich; institutions changing hands and missions; different groups of people excluded, drawn in, pushed out; blocks demolished by fire, reduced to rubble by riots, rebuilt in new configurations. What was visible to my eye reflected hardly anything that had been there just 150 years ago, much less 300 or 1000. There had been layer upon layer of tragedy and opportunity, hard work, injustice, vision, changing populations and changing fortunes. These few blocks, I realized, were a microcosm of similar forces of change over time in lands the world over.

What are we to do with this history beneath our feet? How many of us are living on land that at one time was taken from others by force? How much are we benefiting from events that brought unspeakable loss to others? If there are themes of injustice or discrimination—or genocide—in the history of our people and our place, we need to take those in, and consider whether there is work to be done in the present to make something that has been broken whole. In a very real way, we ourselves cannot be whole until this happens.

In another real way, however, we occupy this place in time and space by chance. Each of us came into this world without choice, and without sin. It is not ours to take onto our shoulders all the wrongs of history and, much as we might wish to, we cannot change the past.

To find our way through this paradox, perhaps we can learn from those who came before. I think of the stories I've heard about our native people, how when they killed a deer to eat, they would give thanks for the life of that deer. It was a promise to honor the spirit of that which was sacrificed to give them life. Is there a similar way that we can honor the lives that were lost and damaged, upon which our lives in the present have been built?

I think of the tiny plot of land in the community garden where I now grow vegetables—and consider the layers. On top is the good rich soil that I have built up over the years. Underneath is the rubble of a burnt-out warehouse, the end of a business on a city street that was once a turnpike between towns. It was likely a field before then. And before then, there was forest—sustaining the lives of earlier humans, and before then animals, and before then…

Perhaps the best I can do is to remember all of these things, and know that there is no way I can have any real ownership of this bit of our planet. What I can do is contribute to the integrity and beauty of this layer in this time, hold it with great respect, open myself to the possibility of sharing it with someone whose claim is as good—or who may need it more—and give thanks for the gifts it brings to my life.

Pioneers

I've always struggled when the conversation turns to ethnic identity. My family has been in this country so long that it's hard to name anything outside of some generic connection to the British Isles. I remember the surprise of visiting my husband's Pennsylvania Dutch relatives and discovering that they, and the whole community around them, had distinctive foods, expressions, art forms, and customs—something that seemed totally lacking in mine.

I've had a similar struggle around reclaiming language. I love language, and would love to reclaim one but, so far as I know, my family has always spoken English. Yet there's a big idea here that resonates with me: in order to think well about people from other countries, and about the larger environment, it helps to have some emotional connection to "home" and "people" ourselves.

I had the opportunity in a small group recently to explore this issue of claiming our people. My grandparents grew up on dirt farms in the Midwest, and I've always felt a connection with the pioneers. I particularly love pioneer women, with all their strength, resilience, creativity, versatility and capacity to work hard. My grandmother is the one I knew who was closest to that experience.

I remember how she taught us as children to weave rag rugs, using long balls of rag strips and working the simple but serviceable loom that my great uncle had figured out how to make for her. What a great lesson in competence, thrift and agency! What a heritage to treasure!

As I thought of my great-grandparents settling in Kansas and Oklahoma, suddenly, and for the first time, I made the connection with my history lessons. I remembered the image of covered wagons lining up on the Oklahoma border, ready to stake a claim to the newly-available Indian land. These good people, my people, were taking land that was available because the native people were being removed.

The earliest story that's told of my family, probably from the mid-1800s, is of a premature baby who was bundled into a feather comforter and put in the wagon heading west and who, amazingly, survived. It's a story of resilience. So now I'm thinking, they were living in Ohio or Indiana, which used to be indigenous land, and they're heading west, as native people are being pushed farther off the frontiers.

In an earlier effort to try to breathe some life into who my people were, I found a book in the library of letters from a Quaker woman who moved from Maryland to eastern Ohio in the 1820s. She talks about how hard her husband worked grubbing stumps out of the earth, so they could plant their crops. And now I'm thinking, those were the eastern woodlands that some group of native people loved and called home.

It grieves my heart. While they may never have personally killed Indians, there they were, right in the middle of a genocidal movement across the country. I can't give up on the goodness of my people. Those qualities that I have cherished, and that were significant in shaping who I am—strength, resilience, love of good work, an ability to put hand and mind together to create something new, an appreciation for the gifts of the land — can still be cherished. But the story of my people, working to create good lives as they moved west, cannot be separated from the unbearable losses suffered by the natives of this land as a result of that movement. Somehow, I have to hold them both.

I've known for a long time that we need to do a better job of coming to terms with our nation's history of genocide, but it's been a theoretical understanding. Now, as I reach to claim my people more fully, it has become something real.

Access to the fast lane

Our city expressway is among the oldest in the nation, and our short local ramp is a challenge, providing easy access only at the best of times. Yet it serves as an unexpectedly powerful metaphor on the relationship among speed, access and equity in our world.

When there aren't many cars on the expressway, there is no problem. The spaces are wide, cars on the ramp are already in motion, and anybody can find a way in. When there's more than enough to go around, everyone can get what they need.

When the expressway is so crowded that everyone is already moving at a crawl, then those on the ramp simply edge in. The distinction between fast lanes and ramp has disappeared and it's like one giant merge. Everyone takes it as a matter of course that they will have to yield to someone on the ramp. If we're all in the same situation, then we acknowledge our peerness and our common need, and all work together to move forward.

Yet when the expressway is full of fast-moving cars, getting on from the ramp becomes an incredible challenge. Most of those who are zooming along pay no attention to the line waiting to get on. Moving speedily on their way, they are happy to be experiencing no difficulty, and not inclined to make any for themselves. Even if someone would choose to make space, when the passing lane is full it is not easy to do. Slowing way down requires entrusting your safety to the reflexes of many drivers behind you (as well as incurring their wrath), and still may not offer a big enough gap for the cautious person on the ramp who has to proceed from a complete stop.

The more speed some of us have, the harder it is for the slower ones to get in. In no way are those on the ramp less deserving of speed. Nor do we have any particular right to our speed; we just happen to be already on the expressway.

Equity will only be achieved when the expressway becomes so crowded that no one has an advantage, or when those of us with the speed decide together that there are some advantages for us as well as for others in slowing down, or if we put resources into a massive redesign of the whole system to allow equal access to those fast lanes.

Drilling for truth

There are at least three quite different ways of seeing the issue of race and racism—all of them true. There is the lens of our personal experience: the messages we got as children, the people we have known, the experiences we've had, the things that have stretched and moved us, the things that have been hard.

Then there is the lens of history and society: the impact on Black people of slavery followed by over a century of government-sanctioned discrimination, the current reality of segregation and inequality, the growing barriers to immigration, and attitudes about race that range from passively unaware to actively hostile in much of the population.

Then there is the third lens of the Spirit: the understanding that ultimately, we are all children of God, that in the most profound sense race is an artificial construct that serves to divide people who belong together.

If we think of these as three layers, one on top of the other, most of us tend to relate to one of them more than the others. With the top layer, we see race personally, our own experience is our primary reality, and everything else seems too far away, too abstract. With the middle layer, we are acutely conscious of the enormous damage of institutional racism and feel that the main job has to be exposing that reality. With the bottom layer, we cling to, and hope to rest in, the knowledge that we are all one, and can't imagine anything more fundamental.

I think much of our difficulty in addressing issues of race and racism comes from trying to communicate with the folks who relate to a different layer than the one that so clearly reflects reality to us. We get so frustrated. Those other folks seem so insular and blinkered, or so grim and guilt mongering, or so simplistic and other-worldly. I think there's a solution though. It lies in moving from the horizontal to the vertical, inviting everybody to get together on top of the whole thing and start drilling.

Drill into that layer of personal experience. Remember what we were told when we were little, who we had access to and who we didn't, who we loved, what was hard. Tell our stories to each other. Drill a little deeper into that layer. Reflect on how our experience has shaped our attitudes toward race. Dare to celebrate our loves and our deep connections. Dare to imagine how naïve unawareness can be experienced as hurtful and seen as racist. Nobody is bad here—it's just a rich opportunity to uncover more and more truth. It's an important layer where we could spend a lot of time, but there's more below.

Drill into that hard layer of institutional racism. Learn about slavery, about the tragic long-term impact of a corrupted and aborted Reconstruction, about how discriminatory lending policies made it almost impossible for Black Americans to build wealth through home equity till well after World War II, about how structural racism continues to segregate and bar equal access to education, jobs and health care. Share what we learn. Be willing to grieve. There's way more here than any of us want to fully take in. But until we get through this layer, until we interact with this truth, we don't have full access to what's below. We can imagine the good clean water down there. We can talk about it. But we can't drink it.

Only when we've done the hard work of drilling, through the cloudy water of personal experience, through the bitter water of institutional racism, only then will we be able to drink the life-giving water of oneness in the Spirit, the deepest truth of all.

Turtle island

This is a story about an old stone turtle in our neighborhood park, a pre-dawn walk with a one year old, and the Standing Rock Sioux nation's struggle to stop a pipeline that threatens their river and sacred sites in the Dakotas.

I've known this turtle for a long time. My boys, who used to play at the little wall and slide surrounding it, now have children of their own. While the rest of the playground was torn down years ago to make way for a bigger, fancier one across the street, the turtle has stayed. The Standing Rock nation is new to me, though I have been following stories of indigenous leadership in protecting the environment for several years. I've cheered their efforts from afar, as a well-wishing onlooker needing all the hope I can get in this scary world.

But after spending five days kayaking from the Six Nations reserve in southern Ontario to Lake Erie, in a joint effort to honor the treaties and protect the earth, that well-wishing onlooker role no longer fits. It's personal now. With the tension growing around the pipeline standoff, the drum-beat of urgency grows: People are being brutalized by pipeline security guards. Rights are being flagrantly abused on all sides and no one is listening. If you care, you've got to do something. Get yourself out to the Dakotas. Drop everything you're doing to organize everyone you know to stand against this injustice.

I'd like to. My heart is pounding along with that drum. But I don't see how I can drop everything I'm doing, and something keeps me from seeking out videos of oppression and details of injustice, sharing with all my friends, and urging them to watch and share as well. I just don't see how more free-floating outrage, laced with despair, numbness and guilt, will help.

So, when I get a note from a new friend on the Six Nations reserve that they will be holding a sunrise prayer service Labor Day morning to support the people of Standing Rock, and inviting me to join from a distance, I know I want to be there. These are people I know and love. This would be a way to connect. But I had offered to take our two young grandchildren Sunday night, to give my son and daughter-in-law a break and help her heal from a nasty concussion. Even with the help of my husband, I have no idea what will be required of me at dawn.

But the one-year-old is awake at 5:30, ready for a new day. So we get up, gather clothes for the cool of the morning, collect the stroller, and head down to the park to greet the day. As I wonder where to settle, I remember the turtle. With me sitting on the ground and him content in the stroller, it's a perfect spot. We stroke the rough places and the smooth places on the turtle's back and head, and I talk to him about why we are here. I talk about Turtle Island, the name local indigenous groups gave to this land, about how we love the earth and the water and the air, how we need to protect it, about the people of Standing Rock and our friends at the Six Nations reserve, how we're all in this together. We play with the spiky little balls from a sweet gum tree. And the sun comes up. And in the sweetness of this time together, my eyes fill with tears.

This was the missing piece. One of the great gifts of the summer kayaking trip had been a story that an elder shared from her grandmother: You have to cry till your tears run sweet. With those tears, I can remember not just what is urgent, but what I love.

The next evening, I hear from one of our other new friends. She is heading out to the Dakotas to serve as a medic in the pipeline struggle and looking for support. This I can do, and I'm glad for the opportunity to do it. I'm thankful to these precious friends and wise ancestors, to a bright-eyed grandchild, and to that old stone turtle, invisible to me in the park all those years, for helping me find a way to do my part.

Town hall

When we arrived at the neighborhood rec center for the town hall meeting, almost all the seats were already filled. More and more chairs were being brought in to accommodate the growing crowd, and still people were left standing. Clearly the topic of cash bail hits a nerve in this neighborhood.

The town meeting was hosted by two progressive-minded city and state legislators. They had invited our new District Attorney, the head of the Defenders Association, a Mayor's representative on criminal justice reform, and representatives of several community organizations that are working to end cash bail.

The feisty determination of both the new DA and the Public Defender to change the system was heartening. I kept being surprised at how neither of them (a white man and a black woman) sounded like politicians or bureaucrats; it was more like they were zealots on a common mission.

The crowd was certainly with them, ready to be led and ready to pull them ahead even faster and farther. It was this crowd—and my part in it—that really caught my attention. I'm still puzzling over how I could have remained so deeply ignorant of the impact of this issue for so long. I remember disagreeing with the policies of an earlier DA with a reputation for being "tough on crime," but now I was hearing from a mother in the row directly behind us about her son who was locked up at age 15 by this DA many years ago and has been in jail ever since. She is my neighbor. How could I be so insulated from her pain?

In this room, only a mile from home, I was finally experiencing the raw reality of the weight of mass incarceration in my community. It was the difference between having information about wrongs and being witness to them. Three mothers spoke, clearly in a never-ending and passionate quest for justice for their sons. How had I failed to be under the weight of this injustice, failed to take into my heart how families are still being ripped apart by a system that started with slavery and morphed almost seamlessly into mass incarceration?

I remember the shock of learning several years ago how towns like Ferguson, Missouri, fill their coffers by extorting traffic fines from their minority neighborhoods. I am embarrassed that I have only recently educated myself on cash bail—a system where the innocent poor can languish in jail for months waiting for trial while the guilty rich simply buy their freedom. But this evening we learned together about another layer of injustice; we learned that 30% of all posted bail is kept by the city—whether the person is taken to trial, proved innocent or not.

I was present as the reality of this outrage took shape and gained weight before our eyes: the meager resources of those who have the least are being pillaged to support the system that oppresses them.

We didn't know. Even the City Councilman, a guy who said he might have ended up in jail himself if somebody hadn't offered him another path, didn't know. How could we not know these things? What forces have allowed us to accept such a system as inevitable? Are those who have been victimized by it too inured by oppression and injustice to speak up? Are those who haven't been personally touched by its horrors too buffered from inconvenient truths, or too invested in not knowing?

Learning and knowing hard things can be painful. But we don't have to learn or know them, or act on what we have learned, alone. And choosing to not know is way worse. The opportunity to be with my neighbors as we looked squarely at this system together, and united in an intention to change it, was a gift.

6

Earth

Sunrise and spring

This late April day is cold and raw, with a biting wind. In my winter jacket, I pull the scarf around my head, and brace against the wind. I tell myself that it can't go on forever.

I'm reminded of a winter long ago that wouldn't give up its grip. Finally, my mother decided that we had to do something about it, and we started organizing a "Welcome Sweet Springtime" party. We pulled great sheets of brown paper off the roll and painted the most springlike pictures we could imagine, full of color and flowers and birds. We hung them all over the downstairs of our house, along with a great banner saying "Welcome Sweet Springtime." We baked a cake and decorated it. We sang songs of spring and life and hope. And sure enough, spring finally came around.

Another time of great anticipation in our family's life was the Easter sunrise service. My parents would wake us up in the deep darkness of pre-dawn, we would bundle up and gather together our warmest blankets and car robes and head out in the night to the home of a family in our Quaker meeting who lived above the Hudson River. Arriving, still in the dark, we would join others, finding our way past the house, up a path and to a little clearing in the woods. There we would lay down the car robes, wrap ourselves in extra layers, and settle in to wait for the dawning of a new day.

It was always a magical time. We listened for the first bird song, then heard the chorus begin to swell. We were present as the darkness of the night began to thin, and the details of the world began to emerge in the growing light. Our attention went to the river, as the colors in the sky became more and more concentrated on one point — then out of that point, the sun emerged. Our service over with the risen sun, we went down to the house for breakfast, then home to more traditional Easter activities. But bunny rabbits and chocolate eggs could never really compare to that shared experience of rising in the night and witnessing the coming of the day.

I'll never forget the year we waited and watched, and the sky grew light and day came but there was no sunrise for us to witness. Deep layers of cloud hid it from sight. And though that could have been a cause for disappointment for a child, it turned out to be an unexpectedly profound moment for me. We couldn't see the sun, but it was still there regardless, rising up from the horizon, shining as brightly as ever behind those clouds. The fact that we couldn't see anything didn't affect the reality of what was there.

The sun comes up. Winter turns to spring. We love and are loved. Paying attention and celebrating help us to notice and appreciate these truths, but whether we experience them in the moment or not, they are still true.

Weather dance

After a hard rain that wreaked havoc with a local fair, it was easy to wish that we could mandate good weather. But I remembered a cautionary tale from my childhood about a prince and his magic rain cloud. He could produce a storm at any time, but there was always somebody who pleaded for sunshine at that moment; he heeded their pleas, and the land got dryer and dryer (though of course the story ended up with a good rainstorm). It's probably just as well that the government doesn't manage the weather, but we do chafe at not having more control.

I guess it's because we've figured out so much about controlling the weather, at least indoors. We've mastered so much that we feel entitled to mastery — so life can go on every day just as we've planned it. It's shocking, somehow, not to be in control of the weather. Surely an advanced, technological, affluent county such as ours shouldn't still be subject to something so primitive and elemental. It just doesn't seem right. So we compensate, by proving how cold we can make it in the summer, how hot in the winter. It would be more rational (and way more fuel-efficient) to find an indoor temperature that everyone would agree on for all seasons. But I'd go even farther. I'd advocate for some of the pleasures of difference that we've lost in our drive for uniformity of comfort.

This would mean rebuilding our relationship with the weather. It would mean rediscovering the cycles of the day and of the year: getting up earlier in the heat to enjoy the cool mornings, slowing down in the afternoons, drinking in hot summer evenings filled with crickets and fireflies, filling up the house with cool night air. It would mean learning the art of dressing in layers, looking forward to the joys of snow, warming chilled hands in front of a fire (or a space heater), eating hearty soups, really appreciating the heat in a cup of hot tea or cocoa. It would mean tolerating some discomfort. There may be times to insulate ourselves in climate-controlled cocoons, but if that becomes our world, we lose one that's so much bigger.

It would mean rediscovering our niche in different regions. I think of the "salt box" houses that developed in New England. The north-facing side had a steeply sloping roof, no windows and plantings of coniferous trees to hold insulating snow and keep out cold winds. The south side had space to accommodate many windows, and deciduous trees to provide leafy shade in the summer and let in lots of winter sun when their leaves were gone. Yet now, houses of that shape are put up all over the country, facing every which way, and trees are purely for show. We have strayed so far from our roots that we don't even notice. Interchangeable styles have replaced the elegance of function and relation to place—and it is a loss.

Of course, weather is not totally benign. There will be periods of oppressive heat and cold, tragic weather disasters. But if we're in opposition and vying for control, the effect of these occasions will likely be bigger. We need to learn to be a partner, leading sometimes perhaps, but many times just following— getting into the rhythm and learning the pleasures of the dance.

Growth dilemmas

It's hard not to have a love-hate relationship with growth. On the one hand, everybody wants things to grow. We nurture little children, coax seedlings into healthy plants, incubate new businesses, invest in emerging talents, all with the hopes that they will make it big time.

Yet growth can be a problem. It's not always true that if something is good, more of it must be better. My six-foot five son is relieved that he has finally stopped getting taller. Enormous impersonal consolidated high schools are now being broken up into smaller units more conducive to human interaction and learning. And we would do anything to stop those cancer cells from growing.

How do we balance these two truths about growth? It's easiest with children and other living things, where we don't have a whole lot of control. They will grow, for the most part, until they are at their mature size, and then they'll stop. Some mysterious internal mechanism knows when they are big enough, when more growth would actually hinder their long-term ability to survive.

But with our human-made institutions, we have no such internal regulator, and our deeply culturally-embedded belief that bigger must be better is getting us into more and more trouble. Nowhere is this more true than in the economy, where growth has become enshrined as a central, unquestionable, quasi-religious, belief. Our well-being, we are told, is dependent on an ever-growing economy: more markets, more consumption, more loans, more debt, more hedge funds on Wall Street.

Yet this economic system is looking less and less like a little child that needs to grow, and more and more like a seven-foot person who's having trouble fitting into ordinary spaces and showing no signs of slowing down—more and more like a cancer growing out of control.

The idea of continuous growth inevitably runs into the limits of the system that contains it. Our growth economy is running through the stored wealth of a finite planet, paying dividends in the present by running up debts against the future, while becoming ever less effective in meeting people's real needs. We find ourselves in the surreal situation of being strong-armed into spending ever more money on things we don't really need in order to keep a system afloat that has become unmoored from reality and common sense.

Luckily, there are other ways to think about growth. It doesn't just have to be about being bigger. After all, we have confidence that our children can continue to grow after they reach their full height. We look forward to them becoming smarter, more able, more mature, even wiser. It's harder with the economy. We've accepted growth in this area as a good thing for so long that it seems like a law of nature. But nature is crying out against it, and what we have made, we can change. (Though our economic high priests could use some help from ordinary folks here—like the child who pointed out that the emperor had no clothes.) We can trade in this outmoded model centered on bigger for one centered on smarter, cut out the cancerous growth, and start learning all the joys as well as the challenges of finding our place within the constraints of a finite planet.

Containers

As I put my lunch into a plastic bag, I wonder what we will do when they are gone. They are so convenient—though I heard somewhere that their average useful lifetime is twenty minutes. How did people use to carry things anyway? My mind goes to my wonderful mother-in-law, wiry and active at 93, taking her basket to market. Now that's a different kind of container.

And there are other containers. I think of Evelyn. For years, a group that my husband and I gathered together as a little non-profit to support the school of a dear friend in Northern Uganda has been meeting over dinner at her house. While everyone brings food, she always cooks a main dish, makes sure there are drinks, thinks where we'll be most comfortable to eat. She recently wondered if she was pulling her weight as a board member. None of the rest of us had a doubt. She was seeing to the container, reminding us that we are family — each one welcomed, each one valued, each one deserving of attention.

For years I was chair of the board of a community organization that faced a constant struggle to survive. Our meetings were full of bad news. So, I always started with sharing good news from our lives and the world around us. We got to know each other better, celebrating each other's milestones and successes, strengthening the container that was our board, so it could hold all those challenges without cracking.

Our bodies are containers for our days on earth. Our neighborhoods are containers for community. Our natural environment is the container that holds us all. What are we saying when we make our containers disposable, when we throw them away heedlessly, when all our attention goes to what they hold?

Some of the things that go into those plastic bags and Styrofoam trays and cardboard boxes support life, I'm sure. Some of the work done at all those meetings where task is valued above all else must benefit humanity. But there is a distortion, a tendency toward short-term thinking, a disregard for what matters and what lasts, that does not bode well.

My mind goes to Evelyn warmly welcoming each one of us into her home, and to the beautiful and sturdy baskets that have hung on the nail in my mother-in-law's basement stairwell for as long as I can remember. You think about what you put in those kinds of containers—and it's not likely to be crap.

It will take some adjusting when I no longer have an endless supply of throw-away bags at my disposal. I don't quite know how I'll manage. But I'm pretty sure it will be good for my soul.

Finding home

A trip to the southwest brought me a revelation about home. The countryside was stunning, but I couldn't imagine living there. Was it the rest to the eye that came with the rolling green and gold hills of the northeast? I hadn't realized until then that I belonged to a bioregion.

I had pegged a friend as a life-long Bostonian, then learned that her roots were in a remote part of Washington state where her father had been a ranger. She spoke with great passion of her connection to that place, then went for a visit and noticed how she relaxed there. As she fantasized about moving back, the fantasy began to gain substance. The last time we talked, she was preparing for the final move. Finances would be tight, but she was going home.

At a focus group on open spaces in my urban neighborhood, as a dozen strangers talked about outdoor places we loved, everyone mentioned the local park. Hardly a bioregion, spanning just two blocks, this is a place that people experience and appreciate in a variety of ways, but the sense of connection and belonging is the same.

Where we feel most at home may be not a place, but a shared religious tradition, a language or ethnicity with associated food and holiday traditions, an age cohort with lives shaped by the same external events, or a common formative background experience. Whether we know them or not, the people in these groups are familiar, comfortable, and understandable. They are our people, we are at home, and we rest in a sense of belonging.

In a way, it's paradoxical. To feel more at home among one people may seem to promote othering. But if we can fully experience being at home for ourselves, then it becomes easier to want that for others. The homes we find may be particular, but the process of claiming and being nourished by a home is universal.

Feeling that we are home, that we are connected and belong somewhere, seems to be fundamental to our capacity to care effectively about our larger home, the earth. How can we claim it as ours, in good times and bad, for better or for worse, if we have no place to stand? If we are skittering across the surface of life as isolated individuals, the little rootlets we try to put down may not provide enough hold to support us well in times of turmoil and trouble. The roots of a home are deeper.

To absorb the strength of that connection, we may need to grieve. I recently heard the story of a woman who has consistently acted on her deep caring for the world, but has been driven by great feelings of urgency, struggling to relax and feel connected while facing what's happening to the earth and its indigenous people. Remembering the story of grandparents who had hung on to their ancestral language, she has been listening to songs in that language and crying, even as she gathers strength from that connection. It seems clear that her reattachment to these roots will serve her well in her work in the world.

I am very thankful to be at home, in my beautiful life-sustaining bioregion, in my well-used and intimately-known city park, in my heritage that stretches back to hardy English farmers, in the communities I'm part of where our roots grow ever deeper together in a web of mutual support. I have a vision of more and more of us gaining the strength from being at home—in many different places and ways—to care for our larger shared home, the earth, with our love and gratitude transmuting into ever greater power.

Hemlocks

Faced with a looming threat to a beloved hemlock forest in northern Pennsylvania, I couldn't imagine just sitting back and doing nothing. But how can one person take on an invasive insect? The only thing I could think of was to be proactive in planting other trees. So I worked to propagate a flat of tiny slips of larch, cut from the tips of the healthy larch that grows near the hemlocks by the pond.

It didn't work. I must have done some part of the process wrong, and each fresh little green slip eventually dried up and died. But while I was in motion, I looked up the name of the tiny invasive insect that was sucking the life out of these great trees. Browsing the internet, I found not only its name—woolly adelgid—but the name of a group that offered a biological remedy. A new seed began to take root and grow.

I shared this resource with my biologist friend, John, who had first seen the telltale whiteness on the tip of a hemlock branch. He saw promise, and I reached out. They offered an on-site consultation, but only during a narrow window of time in the fall, and only on a weekday. The logistics were daunting, but finally one evening in late October we were on our way.

We hurtled through the night in our little cocoon, taking advantage of this spacious opportunity to catch up on months of news. As we got closer, on narrow roads winding through deep woods, we caught glimpses of the gold of fall in the maples. Then we were there, stepping out into a starry night, opening up a cold cabin at midnight and burrowing under covers. In the morning, there was the luxury of reading by the fire as we waited for the Tree Savers man to complete his two-hour journey to this bit of the woods.

With no cell phone service and no address for a GPS, the directions I'd sent in advance were all we had, but he found us. We walked together to look at the hemlocks around the pond, then back to the cabin to the ones I had transplanted twenty years ago—now big young trees—then down the old logging road, through the fields that are now turning to woods, to the forest in the gorge, where we could hear the stream rushing over the little waterfall. This is one of my favorite places on earth, where you step out of the sunshine into the quiet cool cathedral of towering hemlocks.

I liked this young man. His cousin had invited him into her project when he was just sixteen, he'd gone off to college in environmental science, and now this was all he did. His knowledge about the trees, the life cycle of the wooly adelgid, and the habits of the beetle that survives by eating it, was deep. He was proud of the work they were doing together to breed this foreign beetle and help save hemlock forests all up and down the east coast. And he loved the trees. He would stand back and take in an individual hemlock—admiring its shape, its fullness, its color.

Clearly, we were in good hands. And best of all, we might not be too late. He spoke of seeing miles of devastated hemlock forest not far away, all dead and gray. "But your trees are still healthy," he said. "You've caught it in time."

We came back to the cabin, worked out the beginnings of a plan, and noted the details I'd need to get clarified before presenting a proposal to the larger group. Then he left. And John and I packed our few things and got back in the car for the long ride home.

There was an otherworldly quality to the whole experience— that journey in the dark, meeting a young stranger in the middle of the woods, bearer of the gift of precious good news, then traveling back to our real lives, seemingly unchanged, but carrying that treasure within us. And the message continues to warm my heart. It's good to try, and little seeds can grow to bear fruit. Maybe we're not too late. Maybe we can do this thing.

Loving our mother

A group of us were talking about what we love about this world we live in: the soil and the magic of seeds growing, the way we feel when we're in the water, moonlight, the smells at the beach, spring peepers and fresh breezes. There was a sense of eagerness and relief in getting to share this love so fully and openly.

We don't do it very much. There is so much to fear about what's going on these days, so much to worry about. It feels hard to imagine that any single person could make a difference in the face of the vastness of the earth and all its natural systems. It's terrifying to imagine that we might be destroying the environment that is critical to our survival. Most of us cope by trying to not think about it, by numbing off.

But what we don't face, we can't pay attention to. And where we don't pay attention, we can't notice our connection. It's a terrible irony. Many of us don't know how to face the environmental crisis because it matters to us. And to the extent that we don't face it, we can't tell that we are connected, that we care.

Connection is so important. A lot of the hurts that we carry from our childhood have to do with loss of connection with people we were born to love. It is similarly hurtful to lose connection with the environment, with our mother earth. Being in touch with what we love will provide the best leverage for moving the numbness, fears and feelings of hopelessness that stand in our way and keep us from acting. Getting back to that birthright of connection gets us to the solid ground we need to stand on if we really are going to play a role in saving the planet.

As we love more openly, we may be more able to grieve. This can be about the tiniest thing: a single tree that is cut down, a dolphin that dies, one moment that's hard for our children. We may be more in touch with our rage. We may find cracks in a pervasive feeling of numbed terror, and be able to start loosening our fears. Imagining the possibility that one tiny little thing might change for the better can nourish our hope.

So, our first job and most important job is doing whatever we can to open up our access to those deep wells of love for this mother of ours. How can we hope to make any bigger change if our own personal relationship with the environment is distant or tentative or defended? In that group we talked about what it would mean to just keep paying attention to what we love in the natural world around us. It doesn't have to be hard, or take a lot of time. I thought about the ever-changing beauty of the sky—a part of the environment that is always available to me just by looking up. I thought about the pleasure I get when my hands are in the soil, helping in its incredible capacity to sustain us. As more of us remember to pay attention, as we regain that sense of connection, our lives will be better for sure, and more of our love and intelligence will be available to act on. This, more than anything, is what our mother needs.

CHRISTIAN ALTERNATIVE
BOOKS

THE NEW OPEN SPACES

Throughout the two thousand years of Christian tradition
there have been, and still are, groups and individuals that
exist in the margins and upon the edge of faith. But in
Christianity's contrapuntal history it has often been these
outcasts and pioneers that have forged contemporary
orthodoxy out of former radicalism as belief evolves to engage
with and encompass the ever-changing social and scientific
realities. Real faith lies not in the comfortable certainties of
the Orthodox, but somewhere in a half-glimpsed hinterland
on the dirt track to Emmaus, where the Death of God meets
the Resurrection, where the supernatural Christ meets the
historical Jesus, and where the revolution liberates both the
oppressed and the oppressors.

Welcome to Christian Alternative... a space at the edge where
the light shines through.
If you have enjoyed this book, why not tell other readers by
posting a review on your preferred book site.

Recent bestsellers from Christian Alternative are:

Bread Not Stones
The Autobiography of An Eventful
Life Una Kroll
The spiritual autobiography of a truly remarkable woman
and a history of the struggle for ordination in the Church of
England.
Paperback: 978-1-78279-804-0 ebook: 978-1-78279-805-7

The Quaker Way
A Rediscovery
Rex Ambler
Although fairly well known, Quakerism is not well
understood. The purpose of this book is to explain how
Quakerism works as a spiritual practice.
Paperback: 978-1-78099-657-8 ebook: 978-1-78099-658-5

Blue Sky God
The Evolution of Science and Christianity
Don MacGregor
Quantum consciousness, morphic fields and blue-sky thinking
about God and Jesus the Christ.
Paperback: 978-1-84694-937-1 ebook: 978-1-84694-938-8

Celtic Wheel of the Year
Tess Ward
An original and inspiring selection of prayers combining
Christian and Celtic Pagan traditions, and interweaving their
calendars into a single pattern of prayer for every morning and
night of the year.
Paperback: 978-1-90504-795-6

Christian Atheist
Belonging without Believing
Brian Mountford
Christian Atheists don't believe in God but miss him:
especially the transcendent beauty of his music, language,
ethics, and community.
Paperback: 978-1-84694-439-0 ebook: 978-1-84694-929-6

Compassion Or Apocalypse?
A Comprehensible Guide to the Thoughts of René Girard
James Warren
How René Girard changes the way we think about God and
the Bible, and its relevance for our apocalypse-threatened
world.
Paperback: 978-1-78279-073-0 ebook: 978-1-78279-072-3

Diary Of A Gay Priest
The Tightrope Walker
Rev. Dr. Malcolm Johnson
Full of anecdotes and amusing stories, but the Church is still a
dangerous place for a gay priest.
Paperback: 978-1-78279-002-0 ebook: 978-1-78099-999-9

Readers of ebooks can buy or view any of these bestsellers by
clicking on the live link in the title. Most titles are published
in paperback and as an ebook. Paperbacks are available in
traditional bookshops. Both print and ebook formats are
available online.

Find more titles and sign up to our readers' newsletter at
http://www.johnhuntpublishing.com/christianity Follow us on
Facebook at https://www.facebook.com/ChristianAlternative

Also in this series

Quaker Quicks - Practical Mystics
Quaker Faith in Action
Jennifer Kavanagh
ISBN: 978-1-78904-279-5

Quaker Quicks - Hearing the Light
The core of Quaker theology
Rhiannon Grant
ISBN: 978-1-78904-504-8

Quaker Quicks - In STEP with Quaker Testimony
Simplicity, Truth, Equality and Peace - inspired
by Margaret Fell's writings
Joanna Godfrey Wood
ISBN: 978-1-78904-577-2

Quaker Quicks - Telling the Truth About God
Quaker approaches to theology
Rhiannon Grant
ISBN: 978-1-78904-081-4

Quaker Quicks - Money and Soul
Quaker Faith and Practice and the Economy
Pamela Haines
ISBN: 978-1-78904-089-0

Quaker Quicks - Hope and Witness in Dangerous Times
Lessons from the Quakers On Blending Faith,
Daily Life, and Activism
J. Brent Bill
ISBN: 978-1-78904-619-9

Quaker Quicks - In Search of Stillness
Using a simple meditation to find inner peace
Joanna Godfrey Wood
ISBN: 978-1-78904-707-3